Small
Environments

Contemporary Design in Detail

Small
Environments

Yenna Chan

GLOUCESTER MASSACHUSETTS

ROCKPORT PUBLISHERS

First published in the United States of America by
Rockport Publishers, a member of
Quayside Publishing Group
33 Commercial Street
Gloucester, Massachusetts 01930-5089
Telephone: (978) 282-9590
Fax: (978) 283-2742
www.rockpub.com

Library of Congress Cataloging-in-Publication Data available

ISBN 13: 978-1-59253-231-5
ISBN 10: 1-59253-231-4

Series Editor and Art Director: Alicia Kennedy

Designer: Chris Grimley for over,under

Cover image: Studio Aisslinger, Loftcube
Photograph by Steffan Jänicke

Printed in China

Contents

Introduction

When a recent survey of Andrea Zittel's work arrived at the New Museum in New York City, one wall of the exhibition was given over to the artist's manifesto "These Things I Know for Sure." Two assertions resonate with the condition of living in a small space "It is a human trait to want to organize things into categories. Inventing categories creates an illusion that there is an overriding rationale in the way the world works. What makes us feel liberated is not total freedom, but rather living in a set of limitations that we have created and prescribed for ourselves." Zittel uses the home as a laboratory for experimenting with the questions that arise from often self-imposed limitations. As such, her investigations offer a paradigm for small residential spaces that turn constraints to an advantage, that use the details of design to create a versatile and meaningful living experience derived from a logic of compactness, efficiency, and discreteness.

The designers of the projects collected in this volume have treated size as a condition like any other—topography, climate, density—that might spark a creative response. Where no physical boundaries existed, the designers have applied artificial parameters. And some limits, whether financial or aesthetic or cultural, are always present. Architecture is, in one sense, just a way to organize our interaction with the environment outside, to mark our daily routines, and to make sense of internal experiences. Small spaces require a more rigorous way of thinking: In some of the works featured, the categories of dwelling are distilled into a few essential ideas and functions, establishing a set of boundaries with which the design plays. All these projects show that smallness is not a conceptual limit.

Today, more than ever, the small residential environment serves as an arena for architectural innovation. But far from being a new movement, small, well-designed residences have interested homeowners and architects alike over the last two centuries. As mechanized convenience gradually replaced human labor in the early and mid-nineteenth century, activists like Catherine Beecher publicly advocated smaller and better organized spaces for managing household tasks without domestic help.[1] At the beginning of the twentieth century, the interior designer Elsie de Wolfe dedicated a chapter of her book *The House in Good Taste* to the subject of furnishing and decorating small rented apartments; in it, she acknowledged the apartment typology as the answer to many of the issues surrounding modern urban living.[2] The social housing estates of European modernism, such as the widely known 1927 Weissenhof Siedlung in Stuttgart, tied design to visions of efficiency and modernization to address substandard living conditions and affordable housing needs. Starting in 1936, Frank Lloyd Wright's Usonian houses demonstrated new methods of construction and design to create simple, affordable single-family homes. Their innovations allowed for the mass modernization and standardization, to different degrees, of suburban middle-class housing that followed midcentury with the development of the compact California Case Study Houses, the Eichler Homes, and Levittown.

Other typologies—suggesting ideas of domesticity, mobility, and refuge—provide a historical context for the small architect-designed dwelling as well: the traditional Japanese wood homes that transform space through sliding screens and built-ins, the vacation houses and trailers of mid-century America, and, not to be forgotten, the ubiquitous retreat in the woods. Not surprisingly, the majority of the projects in this book invoke the model of the individually designed modernist house or apartment. Despite the size of the residences, however, which vary from a 6-foot (2-meter) cube to a 1,345-square-foot (125-square-meter) house, the designers have avoided a reductive approach. Neither simply well-designed sculptural objects nor miniaturized versions of a larger dwelling, these spaces make manifest the inhabitants' relation to their environment, often encapsulated in a single room. With an immediacy more like that of furniture or clothing, this architecture is closely linked to the individual, revealing intimate details of the way that he or she lives.

Faced with the need to condense expression and function within a small space, these designers have merged aesthetics with original approaches to the quotidian. Using architectural strategies that consider in a new light the usual elements of circulation, fenestration, cabinetry, or finishes, they instill a sense both of order and of expansiveness. The ingenious design details in these projects look beyond the usual décor-oriented methods of furniture placement. Instead, they create a unified architectural environment through the manipulation of spatial limits and the integration of furnishings, materiality, and space.

The categories by which we have organized the works thus emphasize the experience and use of space rather than formal elements. Confronting limiting physical conditions inside and out, expressing condensed spatial relationships, and ordering the aggregate program pieces required by the inhabitant are the essential challenges. The first section, "Mediating the Outdoors," explores substantive and implied relationships between interior and exterior that expand the space or connect it to its context. The second and third sections present contrasting ideas of transformation and compartmentalization: Projects in "Spatial Boundaries" generate architectural events through the direction of movement

Uni Architects, 15 Clifton Street

Henning Larsens Tegnestue, Summer House

or views within the environment, while those in "Ordering of Contents" create a systematic approach to dwelling through interior assemblies. The last section, "Surfaces and Finishes," looks at the way that surface treatments, with an emphasis on color, contribute to overall coherence and provide spatial definition.

Of course, nothing is static. Some projects might exemplify a particular strategy here even if better known for another aspect of their architectural investigation. Likewise, a number of projects that appear in one section might have as easily appeared in another. The Keenan Tower House would have also been at home in "Surfaces and Finishes," the way its textured base references the bark of the surrounding trees. The Echo Park House, on the other hand, might have fit just as comfortably in "Spatial Boundaries," given the layered plan, with its many ways in which to enter and exit.

These projects also address larger factors, new and ongoing, that affect the size of dwellings. In both industrialized and developing nations, the cost of living, land, and construction continually rises while the amount of available buildable space in cities diminishes.[3] In older urban areas, buildable land is often limited to infill lots with challenging proportions and equally challenging zoning regulations. To address the problem of the housing shortage, designers have continued to work on developments with small, affordable units, but have, at the same time, introduced the idea of adaptability. Modular multiuse shelters, such as those shown here by Sean Godsell and Horden Cherry Lee, are prefabricated to provide greater flexibility in planning and construction time than would an entire planned development, are sufficiently small and lightweight to be transported easily, and are potentially less costly.

While population density and a shortage of affordable housing are not new, certain conditions have changed. The family unit has transformed dramatically in North America and Europe since the era of the Cold War. Smaller or once-atypical domestic arrangements bring with them new spatial requirements. Current lifestyle trends, including the widespread phenomenon of relocating to multiple cities in pursuit of employment, are addressed in the projects of Arts Corporation and Studio Aisslinger. These compact, nomadic residences provide a way to customize rented living space and create a portable home within an expensive urban real estate market. This is but one segment of society that has long been underserved by the design and construction industry, which has typically catered to traditional homeowners. Accordingly, rather than singling out a particular cultural idea of a small home and its associations, the selection of works embraces architecturally inventive approaches toward the condition of compactness that have universal appeal and relevance. So, too, the households of the small spaces in this volume range from an individual to a family of five; their dwellings thus reflect different ways of accommodating the structure of contemporary life.

Finally, house sizes have cycled, consistent with social and economic conditions. Despite the steady increase in postwar dwelling size in North America, an inclination toward smaller spaces has surfaced. In fact, a recent *New York Times* article showed a slowly growing preference for improved amenities over floor area, suggesting a dissatisfaction with the McMansions of the 1980s and 1990s.[4] As exemplars, the projects collected here represent some of the most remarkable residences from recent years that, attentive to our current living conditions, introduce moderation without a compromise to design. There is contentment to be found in smallness, and contrary to Robert Venturi's rejoinder to Mies van der Rohe, "Less is a bore,"[5] these small environments possess an abundance of complexity and depth, even when they appear minimalist in spirit.

Notes

1 Catherine Beecher's *A Treatise on Domestic Economy for the Use of Young Ladies at Home and at School* of 1841 included plans for small houses to illustrate ideas of efficient housekeeping. For a more detailed discussion, see Witold Rybczynski, *Home: A Short History of an Idea* (New York: Viking, 1986).

2 See Elsie de Wolfe, *The House in Good Taste* (New York: The Century Co., 1914). Known as a New York society decorator, de Wolfe contributed greatly to the development of the modern interior design industry and was an innovator in transforming the dim, ornate interiors of the Victorian era into the simple and bright spaces of the twentieth century.

3 Half of the world's population lives in urban centers, in multiple dwelling units with no land at all: "In the coming decades, almost all of the global population growth will occur in the cities of the developing world and unless Governments take decisive action to encourage expansion of formal low-cost housing developments, most of that growth will be in slum areas" ("Human Settlements," *Report of the Secretary-General, Commission on Sustainable Development, United Nations Economic and Social Council*, 10 February 2004, p. 1).

4 Fred A. Bernstein, "Are McMansions Going Out of Style?," *New York Times*, 2 October 2005. During the 1980s and 1990s in North America, living space became a commodity like anything else that could be purchased in the west. The McMansion's emphasis on greater floor area usually meant that the quality of design, materials, and construction suffered. Interest in ostentation resulted not only in redundant spaces but also in large spaces allocated to uninhabited areas such as grand entrance halls.

This area of the housing market is the focus of the architect Sarah Susanka, who has stirred the interest of suburban homeowners through her Not So Big House series (see, for example, *The Not So Big House: A Blueprint for the Way We Really Live* [Newtown, Conn.: Taunton Press, 2001]). Stressing craft, details, and the use of materials that appeal to the senses, Susanka's strategies center on creating a comfortable and harmonious environment in smaller living spaces that are adapted to the inhabitants' individual needs. Her ideas, which address common concerns of middle-class suburban living disregarded by many architects, are directed at an audience not typically reached by high-end design. Although through a very different, more prosaic methodology, Susanka's philosophy in fact broaches some of the ideas in Andrea Zittel's work, urging us to think critically about a specific approach to dwelling and to question our relationship with inhabited space.

5 See Robert Venturi, *Complexity and Contradiction in Architecture*, 2d ed. (New York: Museum of Modern Art, 2002).

Arts Corporation, House-in-1

Mediating the Outdoors

The essential theme of "Mediating the Outdoors" is the expansion of space beyond perceived boundaries. The designers here test visual, physical, and conceptual limits, making them ambiguous and abstract by capturing exterior views, daylight, or more ephemeral still, temporal and celestial conditions that connect the interior space to the external environment. At first glance, the two subsections, "Internal/External Transitions" and "Luminance," would appear to polarize site conditions with panoramic views against the absence of views; or, put another way, open site versus infill lot. In actuality, there is more of a mix: Some of the residences in the first section stand on small urban sites, while some of the houses in the second are found in suburban or rural areas. True, all of the examples are in fact freestanding structures (even if land-locked) and with more free surface area for openings, have benefited from increased opportunities for the interior to interact with the environment outside. But the strategies they advance could also be applied to apartments.

Works in "Internal/External Transitions," overlay internal and external space throughout rural, suburban, and urban contexts. The overlap is most obvious in the urban sites of the Glass Shutter and Diagonal Houses, given the clear delineation of the property edges. Both of these buildings open up to courtyards that expand the interior outward, creating outdoor rooms; these spaces also serve as a buffer to the public space of the street. Japanese houses have traditionally devoted space to a courtyard or garden, regardless of the building's size. For more urban contexts, architects must also consider how the building mediates the threshold of public space, whether in the entrance, street elevation, or relationship to neighboring buildings. The works sited in open contexts address the overlap in more personal or even conceptual ways. Loftcube, the A-Z Homestead Unit, Scholar's Library, Keenan Tower, and Hardanger Summer House all respond to their surroundings. Loftcube and the Homestead Unit are meant as multiple and universal modules that fit any site; wherever they are delivered immediately asserts its place as home. In a project like the Summer House, smallness in comparison to the wilderness is also emblematic. For many small projects surrounded by nature, architects draw the focus outward through carefully placed glazing—often generous and preferably operable. Yet even in the intensely urban Loftcube, distant views are borrowed to extend the visual envelope, thereby increasing the sense of space and reducing the barrier between the inhabitant and the external environment.

Little precedence exists in small residential architecture for the inventive channeling of natural light. The innovative details of the "Luminance" projects, however, introduce exciting new strategies for considering light as a medium in the home. Even where lighting schemes address a specific function, such as the ways the Vejby Summer House and Studio and 15 Clifton Street make use of controlled natural light for creating or displaying works of art, the resulting space exceeds the practical objective. Though most of these residences lack impressive vistas, they remain closely connected to the external world through a heightened awareness of the time of day or year. Each work presents a different method to introduce and filter natural light into the living environment without relying on conventional fenestration, which too often the lack of views and dense site context preclude. The daylighting schemes in the Natural Illuminance and Anderson Houses, which employ translucent materials and skylights, began as a response to these constraints, yet produced projects of extraordinary luminosity.

Light may also be used in opposition to structure, to divert the focus away from the enclosure and to dissolve architectural form. In the North and Anderson residences, strong daylighting, akin to that found in sacred spaces, dematerializes the architecture. In the Anderson House, light draws attention to materiality and creates drama as it grazes the luminous, textured surfaces of the walls and ceiling; in the North guesthouse, the monochromatic white interior provides a constant background for light in flux, which erases the hard boundaries of the room. In these projects, light is a medium and architecture the conduit for its experience. Clifton Street and the Natural Illuminance House incorporate diffuse indirect lighting, as well. Combined with white walls, which reflect pure light in the interior, the lighting levels in the two houses remain even and gentle so that the spaces seem calm and contemplative. With few strong shadows, the low-contrast interiors are well suited for many functions, from reading to working, throughout the day, aided in the evening by artificial task lighting. North, although it often possesses these traits, is more mercurial. Both this guesthouse and the Vejby Summer House frame multiple daylighting conditions in a very limited space and use them to define different areas of activity within. The summer residence—the one nonurban home—is the sole project that actively controls light through lattice doors that act as brises-soleil.

The works in "Luminance" all address an intangibility. The designs are based less on function than on phenomenological principles—the experience of external changes in brightness, color, and temperature—things that are larger than the home itself. For these works that venture into the conceptual dimension, the building serves as a small frame for absorbing natural phenomena, allowing the inhabitant to focus on a specific idea or event. The lighting, siting, and fenestration details could be applied to a larger home as an episode in one room or spread out over much greater volume, but the effect would be diminished: It is the direct, intense experience of the external world occurring in the small moments of everyday living that produces the poetic space.

panorama, façade, territoriality, ingress, urban infill, nomadic, outdoor room, streetscape

External/Internal Transitions

Peter L. Gluck & Partners, Scholar's Library, Olive Bridge, New York

This private library for a scholar of Japanese history borders the forest at a weekend property in the Catskill Mountains. The minimal structure, clad with a cement-board rainscreen, at once offers uninterrupted vistas of the wooded site and seclusion from the rest of the family compound. The 20-square-foot (1.9-square-meter) cube is solidly connected to the ground with a monolithic, windowless base that holds ten thousand volumes in shelves from floor to ceiling and conceals a half bath. Access to the building is through a door on the ground level that blends with the exterior finish.

Above and Right Glass panels at the northwest and southeast corners slide back and stack to open up the building to the outside. Columns, one on each side of the cube, are set back from the building envelope to allow for a continuous band of transparency. A stair behind the work surface leads down to the book storage area on the ground level.

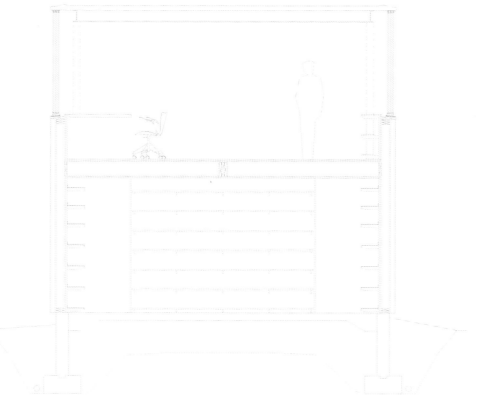

Above The offset metal columns, echoing the vertical form of tree trunks outside, almost disappear. Framed by the visually floating ceiling plane and the linear workstation, the study merges with the woods. The architect juxtaposes the "timelessness of scholarly pursuits" with the fleeting conditions of weather and seasons.

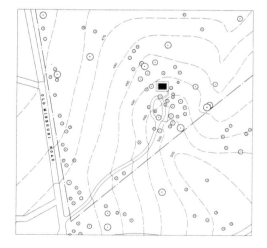

Marlon Blackwell Architect, Keenan Tower House, Fayetteville, Arkansas

Each level of this family retreat reveals a different experience of the surrounding Ozark Mountains: from the wood lattice of the stairwell, to the glass-enclosed observation room, to the open skycourt. The base of the tower, which corresponds to the 50-foot (15.2-meter)-high tree canopy, consists of vertical white oak fins that mimic the textured bark of the oak and hickory trees on the property. At night, light in the base of the tower filters through the lattice to illuminate nearby trees.

Above Rising above the foggy tree line, the over 82-foot (25-meter)-high tower serves as a lookout. Built around an approximately 24.5-square-foot (2.3-square-meter) frame, it is sited on the crest of a wooded hillside surveying 57 acres (23 hectares) of land. Although the tower shares the site with the family's main residence, it is entirely a self-sufficient building. The structure itself recalls a tree house from the owner's childhood.

Above The skycourt is exposed to the heavens. Each wall opening frames the view in a different manner. The formal white wall stands out against the surrounding wooden surfaces, and its immense awning shades visitors from the western sun yet allows for views to the horizon. A table folds up from below the window for dining al fresco.

Right Reminiscent of an observatory, the tower is oriented to the points of the compass and thus augments the effects of solar and lunar movement throughout the year.

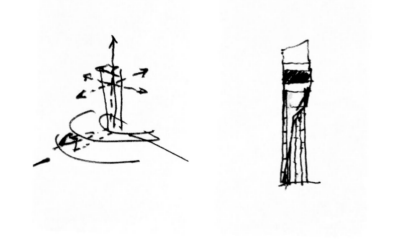

Above A broad slot in the canted wall to the east draws a connection between the striated white oak walls and floors and the dense foliage below.

Saunders & Wilhelmsen Arkitektur, Summer House, Hardanger Fjord, Norway

The architects chose this site for the almost spiritual quality engendered by the bright expanse of the fjord on one side and the penumbra of the forest on the other. The clean, simple forms of the experimental structure create a thoughtful counterpoint to the vivid landscape without ignoring the natural environment. Indeed, situated halfway within the tree line and halfway in the clearing, the cabin tucks its inhabitants into the surroundings while facilitating their experience of nature's vastness.

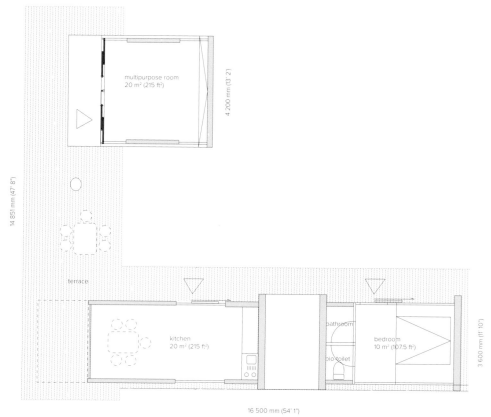

multipurpose room
20 m² (215 ft²)

4 200 mm (13' 2")

14 851 mm (47' 8")

terrace

kitchen
20 m² (215 ft²)

bathroom

bio toilet

bedroom
10 m² (107.5 ft²)

3 600 mm (11' 10")

16 500 mm (54' 1")

Above The house and the platform establish two discrete elements united by common materials. The walls and roof of the single-room cabin are constructed of larch edged with birch plywood; the interior is birch plywood insulated with recycled newspaper. The 14.8-meter (48.6-foot)-long larch platform extends the living space out of doors. From the west comes the sound of waterfalls tumbling into a nearby stream.

Left The architects originally planned for two structures, linked by the long platform: a small 20-square-meter (215.3-square-foot) writing studio and a larger structure that would contain living space, kitchen, bedroom, and bathroom. The project's dual nature is most evident in the proposed plan, as the two buildings and the deck create a more intimate space in the woods where a campfire could be built.

Above The location of the retreat at 80 meters (262.5 feet) above sea level allows for dramatic views over the fjord. Openings cut in the lakeside platform preserve the site's trees, including a mossy tree stump whose poetic form may be contemplated from inside the cabin. This outdoor room serves as a perch from which to take in the nuances of the changing weather and landscape.

Above The unadorned, curving form of the interior wraps around the inhabitant and directs the eye back toward the exterior. In the interest of creating an affordable and minimal structure, utilities are absent; accordingly, the cabin relies solely upon daylight and candlelight. Because the high-latitude location provides about twenty hours of sunlight during the summer months when the cabin is occupied, electricity is not a necessity. Ultimately, the experience of being in the space comes close to the experience of being outside of it.

**Andrea Zittel, A-Z Homestead Unit,
Joshua Tree, California (also no fixed site)**

Located at the artist's studio complex in
Joshua Tree, California, the tiny dwelling
references the Baby Homestead Act of 1938,
which granted five-acre homesteads to set-
tlers who would populate this desert region.
As was typical in historical homestead
grants, the government required homestead-
ers to place a rudimentary house on the
undeveloped land. A spare rectangular cabin
with a corrugated metal roof, the Homestead
Unit expresses the territorial relationship of a
home to its site while evoking the temporal-
ity of these frontier structures. In addition, it
conveys the optimism of the mobile dwelling,
which is ready to be dropped into any location, instantly defining place. Its diminutive
dimensions free the portable module from
the regulations and requirements of a larger,
rooted building.

Above The Homestead Unit may be located indoors as well: Actual applications include the use of the structure as a separate study inside a private home. The dwelling includes three surfaces of varying heights that correspond to sleeping, eating, and working zones. The artist customizes exterior and interior finishes to the individual's requirements. Here, the Homestead Unit rests among Zittel's Raugh foam "furniture" pieces, which constitute an artificial landscape. These synthetic landforms assert a natural order in the interior environment due to their adaptability, unfixed functionality, and expected deterioration. Together, the two create a microenvironment.

Studio Aisslinger, Loftcube, no fixed site

The exterior walls of this 36-square-meter (387.5-square-foot) rooftop unit can be customized using louvered lamellae, clear, tinted, or translucent glass elements, and either solid or perforated materials that provide various degrees of transparency and connection to the cityscape. The Loftcube sits 1.4 meters (4.6 feet) off the roof's surface and, beyond the initial transport and assembly, requires little additional infrastructure: utility connections from the host building and perimeter guardrails for the roof.

Opposite Top This transportable rooftop abode was designed with nomadic urban residents in mind. With unrestricted access to views and daylight, the rooftops of high-rise buildings provide an abundance of potential sites. The architect envisions communities of Loftcube dwellers populating the skyline of major cities. In the evening, light leaking from the base forms a trace of the building on the rooftop.

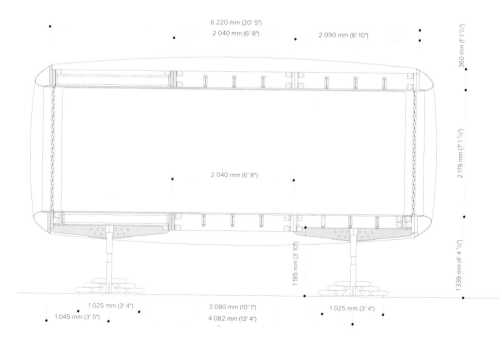

6 220 mm (20' 5")
2 040 mm (6' 8")   2 090 mm (6' 10")
360 mm (1' 1 1/2")

2 179 mm (7' 1 1/4")

2 040 mm (6' 8")

1 185 mm (3' 10")

1 339 mm (4' 4 1/8")

1 025 mm (3' 4")   3 080 mm (10' 1")   1 025 mm (3' 4")
1 045 mm (3' 5")   4 082 mm (13' 4")

Left The four structural base supports are weighed down on the rooftop surface but the structure's own weight also counters wind loads. (The dwelling's design accounts for the typical structural loads of an existing high-rise roof, although each installation would require an engineer's verification.) Augmenting the openness of its sides, a skylight is set into one of the bays of the nine-square grid structure.

Cell Space Architects, Diagonal House, Tokyo, Japan

The approach to this house in a residential part of Tokyo is quiet and restrained; a high wall next to the entrance allows only a small glimpse of the courtyard in front. Corrugated steel panels form the walls of both the house and the fence around the perimeter of the property. The steel-frame two-story house is consistent with the neighboring context, despite its distinct design, as the structure is modest in proportion and neutral in color.

Above Although the house presents a private face to the street, the perimeter wall opens up at the corner to allow a car to maneuver into the crushed stone parking area from the narrow street. The open corner reveals the building on a diagonal with the courtyard, which directs the view back toward the striking façade.

Above The exterior court becomes an extension of the indoor living space as the fence, equal in height to the large opening, takes on the quality of an exterior wall around a square space. At dusk the second level of the house emits a gentle glow through etched glass that allows light but not views into the sleeping quarters.

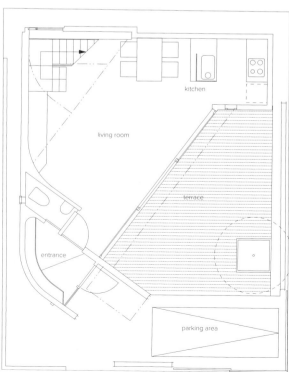

Above The flooring inside the house appears to extend to the exterior even with the glass panels closed. The opposition of the two triangular forms reads as a single space. Above the sliding doors, the glazed wall dematerializes as transom, soffit, and reflected light combine to further erase boundaries between the two sides.

Left In a neighborhood where freestanding houses are built close together, the Diagonal House carves out its own private space on a 107.3-square-meter (1,155-square-foot) site, allocating approximately half of the parcel to outdoor space.

Shigeru Ban Architects, Glass Shutter House, Setagaya, Tokyo, Japan

The simple cubic volume and the shuttered façades develop the familiar architectural language of the commercial streetscape in this busy mixed-use area. Planning restrictions inspired the vertical parti of three tiers that rise toward the rear of the property, accommodating a restaurant, a kitchen-studio, and living space.

Above and Left Despite the narrowness of the site, space is made for a courtyard that provides western light and reorients the building with a second, more private façade. A continuous roof canopy over the stepped floor plates creates a dramatic triple-height space at the front. When the shutters are raised, billowing two- and three-story curtains lend a theatrical quality to the fluid space between street, courtyard, and building.

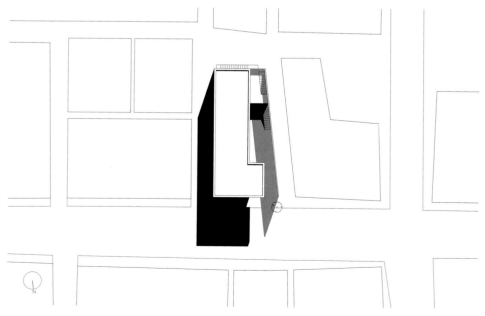

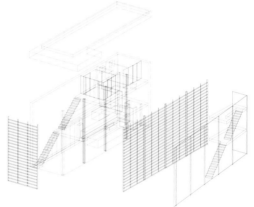

Above and Right With the shutters closed, the bamboo-fenced courtyard changes character. The layered envelope of shutters and curtains provides varying degrees of connection to the outside. A multitude of arrangements—shutters completely closed, shutters opened halfway, or opened along one façade only, with curtains loose or pulled back—constantly transforms the relationship between interior and exterior space.

Opposite The building's hospitable character is revealed when the owner, a culinary scholar, opens up the side along the courtyard to operate the restaurant. With the barrier to the inside lifted, the registration of the human scale allows the courtyard to assume a more intimate nature. Just as exterior and interior are continually brought together or separated, so, too, are the public and private spaces. The idea of adaptability extends to the positioning of the kitchen-studio on the second level where it serves both the restaurant and the living quarters.

translucence, shade, backlighting, direct and diffuse, louvers, skylights reflectivity

Luminance

Endoh Design House with Masahiro Ikeda, Natural Illuminance House, Tokyo, Japan

A grid of 1,200 × 1,200-millimeter (3.9 × 3.9-foot) panels creates ambiguity in the scale of the house and the definition of its edges, making the structure appear larger than its 34.5-square-meter (371.4-square-foot) footprint. Every element in the main space is a consequence of the floating grid, including millwork, storage, and lighting. Five of the solid panels in the living space open for ventilation. Most of all, natural lighting is introduced into the main levels through the lines of the grid. As the illumination levels throughout are uniform, the architects eliminate directional hierarchy in the space.

Above The system of translucent grid and solid squares continues at the ground-level sleeping area, where a lower room height of two squares is the primary indicator of a programmatic change. Because the double layer of squares does not float freely here, the bedroom level feels like an in-between space. A spiral stair descends to the basement level, whose fluorescent colored light seeps upward through the translucent flooring.

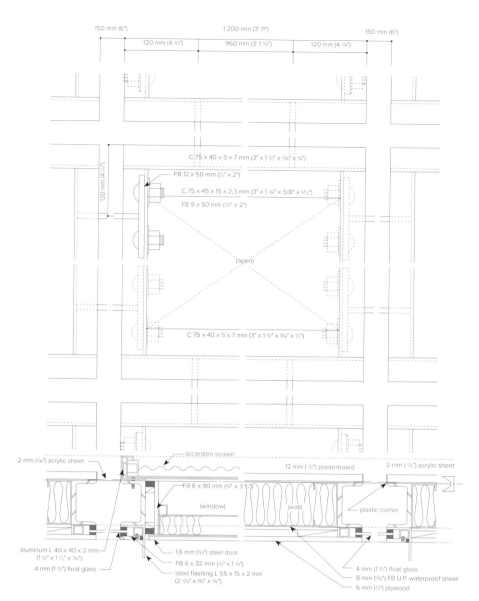

150 mm (6")   1 200 mm (3' 11")   150 mm (6")

120 mm (4 ¾")   960 mm (3' 1 ¼")   120 mm (4 ¾")

120 mm (4 ¾")

C 75 x 40 x 5 x 7 mm (3" x 1 ½" x ³⁄₁₆" x ¼")

FB 12 x 50 mm (½" x 2")

C 75 x 45 x 15 x 2,3 mm (3" x 1 ¾" x 5/8" x ³⁄₃₂")

FB 9 x 50 mm (⅜" x 2")

(open)

C 75 x 40 x 5 x 7 mm (3" x 1 ½" x ³⁄₁₆" x ½")

accordion screen

2 mm (¹⁄₁₆") acrylic sheet

12 mm (½") plasterboard

2 mm (¹⁄₁₆") acrylic sheet

FB 6 x 90 mm (¼" x 3 ½")

(window)   (wall)

plastic corner

aluminum L 40 x 40 x 2 mm (1 ½" x 1 ½" x ¹⁄₁₆")

1.6 mm (⁵⁄₈") steel door

FB 6 x 32 mm (¼" x 1 ¼")

4 mm (1 ½") float glass

steel flashing L 55 x 15 x 2 mm (2 ³⁄₁₆" x ⅝" x ¹⁄₁₆")

4 mm (1 ½") float glass

8 mm (⁵⁄₁₆") FB U.P. waterproof sheet

6 mm (¼") plywood

Above A detail view of the outside corner at the balcony shows the typical grid system of structural square panels held apart and supported by two flat steel bars on each side. The system continues on the interior wall that separates the utility area from the living space. The translucent filler consists of float glass on the exterior and acrylic on the interior.

Above Left The section and plan details show the construction of both operable and fixed units. Each square unit is formed by a heavy steel-channel frame. These are held together, in turn, by implausibly light 9-millimeter (¹¹⁄₃₂-inch) flat steel bars, which disappear against the bright light.

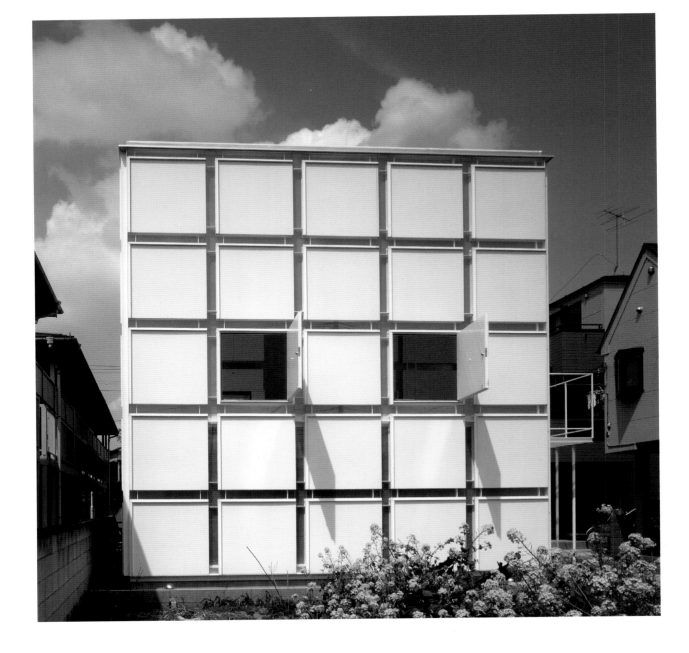

Above Because buildings cluster together on small sites in this densely populated urban residential area, windows can look only onto a jumble of neighboring houses. The Natural Illuminance House creates its own logic by omitting views but not light, with a building envelope that subsumes structure, insulation, ventilation, storage, and fenestration into an unvarying interface.

Opposite In the evening, the lighting effects reverse on the exterior. Strong backlighting makes the solid structure invisible; the grid of light takes on form while the squares dematerialize, reflecting the color of the sky. Once again, illumination renders the building abstract and the scale indeterminate.

Jamie Fobert Architects, Anderson House, London, United Kingdom

Light is the architect's primary medium here and forms the basis of the design. Reached by descending a long, narrow corridor from the street entrance, the main living area, which takes up most of the lower level, feels surprisingly spacious. The building looks back on itself with large high windows open to the court above, where the volume of the guest bedroom is visible. A skylight provides daylight at the other end of the space. With the luminous surfaces and natural wood finishes, the room, although in effect below street level, averts a subterranean feel. In the kitchen, part of the inner structural core of the building, darkness is countered by a wash of light from the skylight above and a linear strip of artificial lighting. Both natural and artificial illumination reveal the subtle texture and reflectivity of the concrete surfaces, for

which the architect developed experimental finish techniques during casting.

Left The site is a landlocked rear lot surrounded by 8-meter (26.2-foot)-high party walls on all sides and accessed only from a 1-meter (3.3-foot)-wide alley between buildings. Rethinking the conventions of fenestration on exterior walls led to the unique design. Adding to the challenge were the designation of the central London neighborhood as a conservation area and the imposition of height limitations on certain parts of the structure to meet daylight requirements for neighboring buildings.

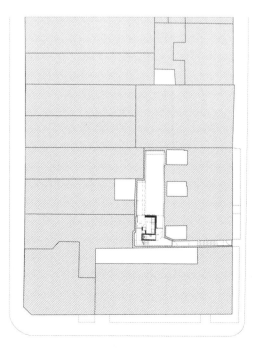

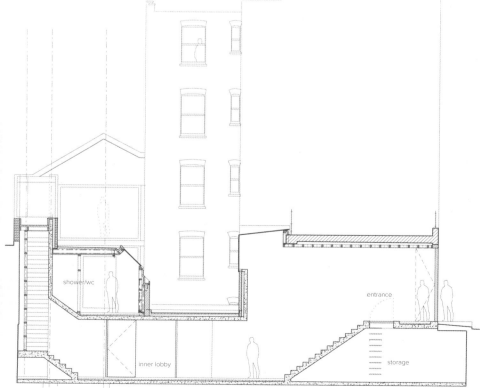

Opposite and Above On the upper level, a freestanding sculptural concrete form in the master bedroom area integrates bathroom components. A translucent panel provides muted light at this end of the space. On the opposite side of the bedroom/bathroom space, a skylight folds over the corner of the gable end. Just out of sight below, an angled wall tilts out to allow another perspective of the court. Built in a complex negative space, the house does not assume a gestalt but dissolves, in the architect's words, into "mass, texture, and light."

Left The section cut reveals inventive lighting strategies used throughout the house, even in service areas such as circulation zones and the guest bath. The two-sided skylight over the entrance stair provides dramatic light for the entry sequence and draws out the view beyond the house. The configuration of these elements produces a strong sectional idea, giving the building an inward focus yet engagement with its context.

shower/wc

entrance

inner lobby

storage

Uni Architects, 15 Clifton Street, Cambridge, Massachusetts

A translucent polycarbonate tunnel between the renovated house and a new addition joins the bright lighting and clean surfaces of the two spaces with its pure, luminous form. The transition is kept as open as possible to draw the flow of space and views to the garden at the rear. At the same time, it creates a solid separation between an outdoor sitting area for the house and the entry area for the rear unit.

Above The open plan of the upper and lower levels of the house make the space feel more expansive while the white finishes reflect light throughout. One side of the house is a functional block, called the "performative wall" by the architects, that concentrates the utilities such as kitchen, bath, and stair. On the opposing side, indirect light falls from a skylight through the slotted opening in the second floor. Although the skylight faces south, the translucent surfaces temper the direct sunlight, providing protected illumination of the gallery of drawings and prints on the wall.

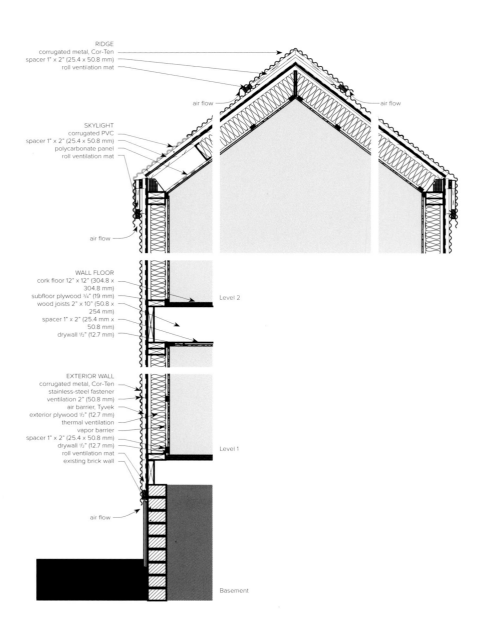

RIDGE
corrugated metal, Cor-Ten
spacer 1" x 2" (25.4 x 50.8 mm)
roll ventilation mat

air flow — air flow

SKYLIGHT
corrugated PVC
spacer 1" x 2" (25.4 x 50.8 mm)
polycarbonate panel
roll ventilation mat

air flow

WALL FLOOR
cork floor 12" x 12" (304.8 x 304.8 mm)
subfloor plywood ¾" (19 mm)
wood joists 2" x 10" (50.8 x 254 mm)
spacer 1" x 2" (25.4 mm x 50.8 mm)
drywall ½" (12.7 mm)

Level 2

EXTERIOR WALL
corrugated metal, Cor-Ten
stainless-steel fastener
ventilation 2" (50.8 mm)
air barrier, Tyvek
exterior plywood ½" (12.7 mm)
thermal ventilation
vapor barrier
spacer 1" x 2" (25.4 x 50.8 mm)
drywall ½" (12.7 mm)
roll ventilation mat
existing brick wall

Level 1

air flow

Basement

Above A typical cross section illustrates the way that the skylight is incorporated into the building: On the exterior, corrugated PVC maintains the texture and form of the Cor-Ten steel, and on the interior, a polycarbonate panel is set flush with the ceiling surface. This provides an individual yet inexpensive alternative to an off-the-shelf skylight product. Not shown in the section is the opening in the joists between the first and second floors, which is located directly below the skylight.

Above Right A closer view of the slot between the first and second levels reveals the wood slats that let light through but retain a usable and stable floor surface. Visually, this feature appears as a continuation of the floor rather than a gap in it, since the slats register as a change in texture.

Above The second-floor space continues the opposition of storage walls and light. From the street, the building does not present visible fenestration other than a single traditional sash window above the door. This window on the rear wall mirrors that on the façade but punctuates a translucent polycarbonate wall. The small window provides more ventilation than light or views. Here, too, the all-white interior increases the brightness and spaciousness of the room.

Elliott + Associates with Michael Hoffner, North, Oklahoma City, Oklahoma

Inspired by the movement of light through the lens of a view camera, this renovation explores the different ways to capture the Great Plains light throughout the day and throughout the year; it also pays tribute to the owner's grandfather, the frontier photographer North Losey. The illumination varies dramatically according to direction, time, and season to produce an atmosphere that flows from the meditative to the otherworldly. Light dissolves form, leaving only the figure of the central square column, a former chimney, with its stelalike slate surface.

Opposite Small details trace the historic context: Throughout the apartment, recessed spot fixtures illuminate vintage photographs on the wall, and a glazed reveal where the column meets the floor gives a glimpse of the garage below. Monochromatic furnishings and surfaces offer an abstract, clean backdrop for the luminous effects, while cool, crisp sandblasted glass panels enclose individual fixtures and functions.

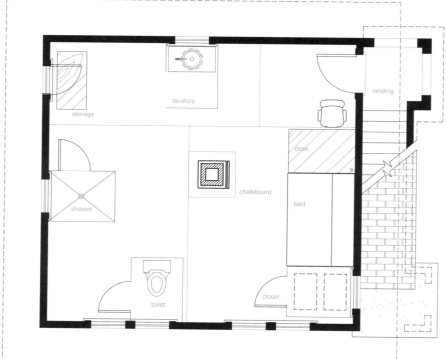

Opposite The architect speaks of the space's monastic quality, a spare, abstract feeling that is bolstered by the absence of electronic devices. Beyond the bed, one of the individual glass enclosures modulates outdoor light.

Above Left One of the windows facing west has an in-swinging mirrored panel on the back of which is applied a holographic film that divides sunlight into the color spectrum. When open during the late afternoon, the panel refracts a rainbow of color into the interior. In this contemplative space, one experiences "the purity of time" and becomes sensitive to variations throughout the diurnal hours.

Left Wood strips on the floor and reveals on the walls and ceiling demarcate the four functional zones of the apartment: entry, dressing, hygiene, and sleeping. The quadrants reference the four cardinal directions and the four seasons so prominent in Native American culture. Consequently, four glass enclosures encase a window on each side of the space. In an unusual arrangement, individual components are broken up and distributed around the apartment as objects within the translucent light boxes. The placement of daily functions in front of the windows on all four sides heightens the experience of the changing light.

Henning Larsens Tegnestue, Summer House and Studio, Vejby Strand, Denmark

Commissioned by a gallery owner, this summer residence and artist's studio is located on an elevated site near a windy coastline. Thus the house opens to the south, where the main living space and front terrace are warmed by the sun and sheltered from the elements. Reinforcing the architects' concept of the house as a tube, a large expanse of low-e glazing spans the full width and height of the south façade. Set in a thicket of ferns, birch trees provide dappled shade.

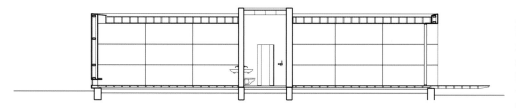

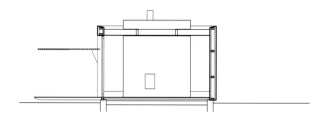

Above On the western side of the building, bays mark the divisions of the program: two main areas that serve as studio and living spaces and a small core containing kitchen, bath, and entry. The long stretch of louvered windows creates a balanced and calm composition that glows at night.

Left The sections make apparent the contrast between the opposing faces of the house, one more open, one more closed, with resultant differences in daylighting. These fixed conditions to the north and south are modulated along the length of the house by the adjustable louvered west wall, while the east wall, containing only the entry door from the road, remains constant.

Above Left The wood panels, constructed of larch louvers and stainless steel angle frame, may be adjusted in both raised and lowered positions using a pair of gas hydraulic pistons on each unit. The larch-strip louvers are hinged at two-thirds of their height to create more effective shading and to provide a more human scale to the abstract form. These horizontal slats align with the larch tongue-and-groove siding. Full-height glazed doors slide behind the louvers on stainless steel tracks.

Above Right The five louvered panels allow for varying lighting conditions in each section of the house and studio. The building is conceptually one volume with a service core in the center, but floor-to-ceiling sliding doors with flush pulls (seen at right) can divide the house into four quarters and further control illumination.

Above The artists' studio occupies the north side of the house, with high and low zones of fenestration. The narrow slot windows provide both indirect light for studio work and seclusion from the street. The northern light casts an even tone on the interior surfaces—birch plywood walls and ceiling and larch floors.

Spatial Boundaries

In a small residence, the essential functions of cooking, bathing, and sleeping along with the conditions of lighting, entry, and circulation must be articulated in a consistent and coherent manner because they are closely juxtaposed. The projects in "Spatial Boundaries" explore the ways in which spaces may be differentiated to create variations of public and private space within the interior of a residence and then the ways in which the spaces are linked through circulation. With a wide range of approaches to partitioning volume, these designers define clear programmatic functions and provide varying degrees of privacy yet also achieve architectural coherence. The layering of spaces sets up boundaries that are then disrupted by visual and thematic connections among spaces. The boundaries do not merely divide an area for separate household functions; they permit often graduated values to be assigned to the spaces, such as more formal or informal, more private or public, and sometimes allow an overlap.

Living environments with dynamic space form the focus of both "Private/Public Functions" and "Circulation." The owners of these residences sought designs that would accommodate multiple uses and experiences, usually in the interest of enclosing sleeping areas without compromising the openness of the overall plan. For, beyond demarcating zones of activity, separations may actually add depth and ambiguity to a space, or create the illusion of largeness. Whereas the projects in "Private/Public Functions" employ horizontal divisions, nearly all the works in "Circulation" concern vertical separations. For the most part, partitions are kept as light and open as possible, but some do double duty: For example, the casework in the Kempenlaan Apartment both divides the space and serves as the home's storage; similarly, the swinging partition in the Convertible Studio uncovers a built-in dining bench.

One of the more difficult design decisions made in a small residence is how and where the separation of spaces occurs. For some clients, even bathroom fixtures do not require enclosure (see the open shower adjacent to the kitchen counter in the T.O. Penthouse in the next section). But for many others, often a family, the dwelling will entail more divisions, especially when addressing an open plan. Artists' live/work studios in former industrial buildings, with their large open spaces, became over time a model for the urban lifestyle; now new developments based on this typology abound. Small spaces, of course, can take advantage of the same features, but their size makes it more difficult to section off areas without diminishing the living space or natural light. The minimal enclosures of the Kempenlaan Apartment and the Healy/Kaplow Loft maintain this light-filled openness without compromising privacy. Visually, the program flows freely from one zone to another. Healy/Kaplow, in particular, with its strategically placed glazing, creates visual and acoustic privacy for a family with an infant.

The Convertible Studio, the Flat in Maida Vale, and the Home/Office for a Graphic Designer contain spaces that transform from public to private. The spatial condition for these rooms is not determinate but fluid, since the boundaries change according to the current activity. These composite spaces transform to accommodate additional functions, in contrast with the transforming elements collected in "Built-Ins and Convertibles," which occur in a more inclusive space. The Maida Vale interior is designed with an open plan, offering flexibility in a living area that may be partly closed off with movable partitions to create a guestroom—a strategy that recalls the retractable and stacking partitions of Gerrit Rietveld's 1924 Schroeder House. In addition, the floating soffits and build-outs at Maida Vale, like Rietveld's abstract planes, create ambiguity in the edge conditions, which provides a sense of expansiveness beyond the room's actual limits.

Another contemporary condition, working from home, leads to the need for a home office. However small the space, most inhabitants still desire some type of separation between living and working. The home office often takes the form of enclosed cabinets that extend the work space into a room during use, then completely close away. With the Home/Office, this separation is not only material but also temporal. The New York apartment is so small that it cannot accommodate another subdivision—this one elegantly forms a wall of the bedroom. Instead, like an either/or, each day the function of the entire room shifts between an office where employees and clients gather to a living space where the owner can entertain friends.

Often, given the dimensions of a plot of land or restrictions on it, the only option is to build vertically. Divisions are no longer a variable but a constant framework. In the projects presented here, vertical circulation links spaces both physically and conceptually, creating a cohesive structure throughout. If one of the rules of small homes is that long corridors are to be avoided, then the stair must be considered as more than a diagonal corridor. The stair may be a compositional element in the design, integrated with similar materials and finishes, such as shown in the Diagonal House, or incorporated into the structural frame of the building, as exemplified by the Small House in Tokyo. The vertical assent may also connect movement through space with the perception of the outer environment, directing the inhabitant to specific views, as do those of both the Small House and the Keenan Tower House. In these projects, every aspect of the stair's configuration—its steepness, geometry, width, whether it is a spiral or straight run, whether or not it has landings on which to pause—conveys the essential nature of the overall design. All of the stairs shown here happen to be metal. This is advantageous in a small space, since metal possesses strength and lightness, requires a small structural profile, and thus occupies less volume; it allows for weatherability and transparency, and contrary to common fears of custom-fabrication expenses, may meet a small budget if it is prefabricated, like that of the Slot House.

Although many of these projects have rather efficient circulation paths, these spaces are not limited to acting as a connector between destinations. One must progress through a residence such as the Slot House to build an understanding of its spaces and character. As the Keenan Tower House and the Reversible Destiny Lofts evidence, the experience of traveling through space can be an event in itself. The Reversible Destiny Lofts, the one project whose circulation lies on the horizontal plane, focuses on the physical and mental aspect of circulation: The sloping, textured floors of its central passage bring a hyperawareness to the sensations generated by the act of walking through the space. Circulation provides coherence to this complex space as it does in the vertical projects: Movement through these spaces is not along the shortest path, but along one that directs attention to the specifics of dwelling in one particular place and time.

screening, duality, seclusion, delimited, directed views, enclose, layering, separation

Private/Public Functions

Studio G+A, Convertible Studio, Jersey City, New Jersey

A large pivoting partition closes off the sleeping area or opens up the living space of this studio apartment. It allows two viewing conditions for the television set, private and public. The translucent material and the holes in the screen intentionally create a moiré effect as light passes through. The partition is constructed from painted wood and corrugated polycarbonate. A large hinge, obtained from a fencing supply company, supports the screen and manages the wires for the television. Cables brace the asymmetrical structure, and a large floor caster on the bottom of the leg allows the panel to swing smoothly.

Right The enfilade of frames at the entry hall creates depth, and a row of closets screens the view of the bedroom area. This hall space serves the dual purpose of a dressing room in the morning and formal reception area when entertaining. The architect likens the parti to a pocketknife, an idea that is carried through in the slightly curved jutting form of the transforming wall.

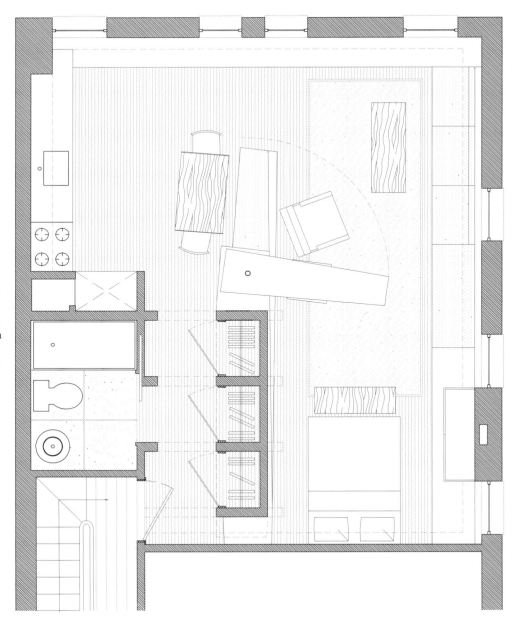

Above When swung out to enclose the bedroom, the partition reveals additional seating at the dining area. Although the studio has just 530 square feet (49.2 square meters) of open space, the transforming element allows for more adaptable uses of the space than would a larger apartment with separate rooms. Keeping the forms and finishes relatively simple but interesting, the designer counters preconceived needs for a larger space to accommodate private and public activities.

Matthew Baird Design, Healy/Kaplow Loft, New York, New York

This loft for a couple with a baby is designed as an open living space that allows some acoustic and spatial privacy for both. The clean, white cube of the bedrooms is the loft's primary form. While enclosed for privacy, the upper master bedroom is generously glazed; its solid walls break before the ceiling to admit plenty of light and to connect it to the rest of the space. Two corners are glazed: The larger one looks outside toward City Hall and the smaller, at the head of the bed, looks onto the interior.

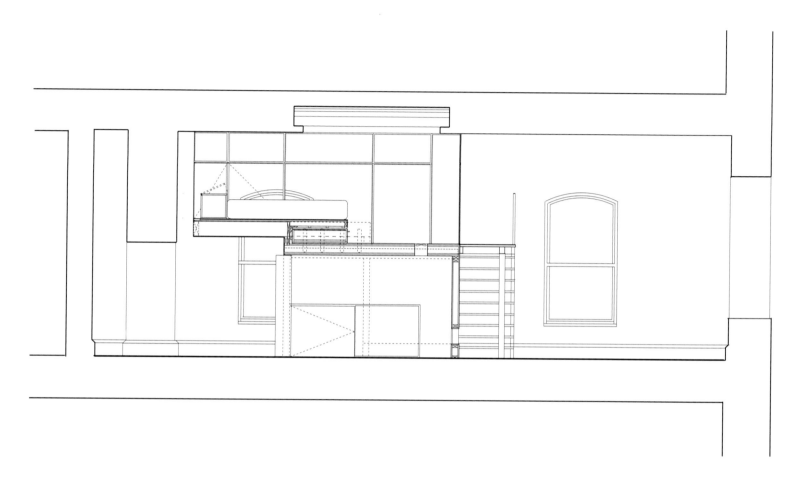

Above The section shows a view east toward the main living space from the bedrooms. In the upper bedroom, the ceiling is excavated to reveal two corrugated steel vaults between the joists that provide additional head room—a fortuitous discovery—as the overall floor-to-ceiling height is just over 14 feet (4.3 meters). Additional space is captured by cantilevering the bed over the hall. The lower half of the cube contains a nearly 6.5-foot (2-meter)-high bedroom with a low, wide door in front that makes it convenient for the parents to check on the baby sleeping in her crib inside. Child-height doors and windows also connect the lower bedroom to the public spaces.

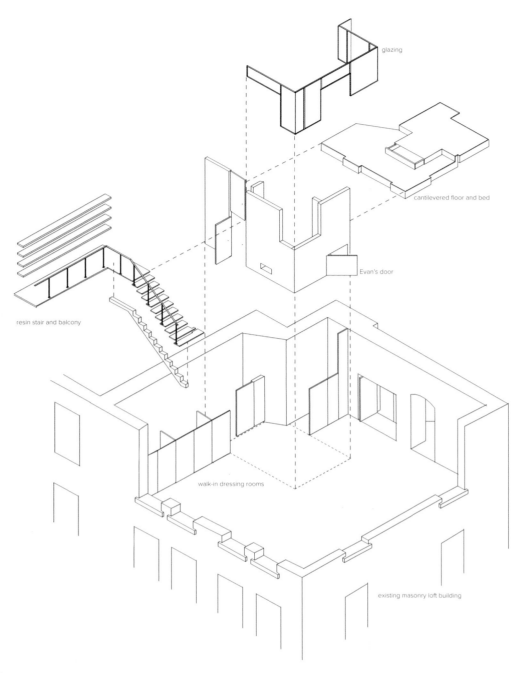

glazing

cantilevered floor and bed

resin stair and balcony

Evan's door

walk-in dressing rooms

existing masonry loft building

Right The addition of the stacked bedroom spaces concentrates the private quarters in the rear of the residence and keeps the living area as open as possible. The bedroom block becomes part of a storage system along the west wall of the loft and reads as part of the perimeter walls rather than as a disconnected object in space. Efficiency of use and economy of material provide organization: The music library above the clothing closets takes advantage of the loft's height.

Above and Left The cantilevered bed also provides spatial definition for the entry sequence. Walking into the loft from the entrance door just beyond the brick bearing wall, one encounters a lower ceiling height that extends the threshold before one steps into the high, open space. The ebonized oak band at the cantilever continues the material of the loft bed inside.

**i29 Office for Spatial Design, Kempenlaan
Apartment, Amsterdam, Netherlands**

To keep the interior spacious yet structured,
the architects approached this apartment
renovation by way of furniture design. A
single piece of custom-built casework organizes the apartment into public and private
zones, yet creates the experience of a larger
open space. The main body of the casework
is spray-finished MDF, which frames an oak
alcove in the living room.

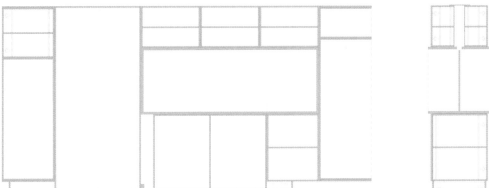

Top The artful placement and composition of the cabinet control the views through the apartment: An opening in the cabinet allows a glimpse of the bedroom area beyond without sacrificing privacy.

Above While acting as a screen, the casework provides the apartment with nearly all its common storage space. In the living area, its lower half accommodates stereo and television equipment and the free end serves as a wardrobe; more storage is accessible from both sides of the unit above the open shelf.

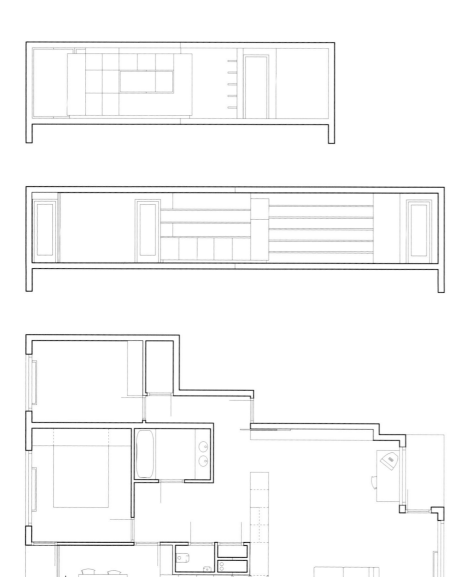

Above Although the cabinet appears as a free-floating object when viewed from the living room, it is in fact integrated with the apartment's interior partitions. The side and rear of the block reveals its functionality, with integrated kitchen and storage elements that wrap around a core containing a washroom and closets. The cabinet creates layers of space that progress from open to more closed.

Above The casework turns into a galley
kitchen as it continues around the corner,
unifying the separated dining and living areas
and delineating the area for entertaining.
Despite the full-height utility core occupying
the center of the apartment, the appearance
of the cabinet through the doorway in the
dining room implies the continuity of space
and reinforces the feeling of openness.

Jonathan Clark Architects, Flat in Maida Vale, London, United Kingdom

The objective of the design of this apartment was flexibility. The architect-owner wished to accommodate guests hospitably without sacrificing space to a room that would be mostly unoccupied. The built-out storage wall between living and dining areas reinforces the perception of the living area as one uninterrupted space. In fact, a barely perceptible seam marks the track for sliding panels that turn the dining room into a private guestroom. The space even triples as a home office, as one of the closets hides a workstation that pulls out into the room.

Above Floor-to-ceiling acoustic panels, supported by a ceiling track, were adapted from a commercial partition product used in conference rooms. When stacked into an alcove, the panels become flush with the thick wall, which also stores a fold-down bed. With the panels in use, the alcove reveals a door to the newly created bedroom. The dining table moves into the living room when the room is enclosed.

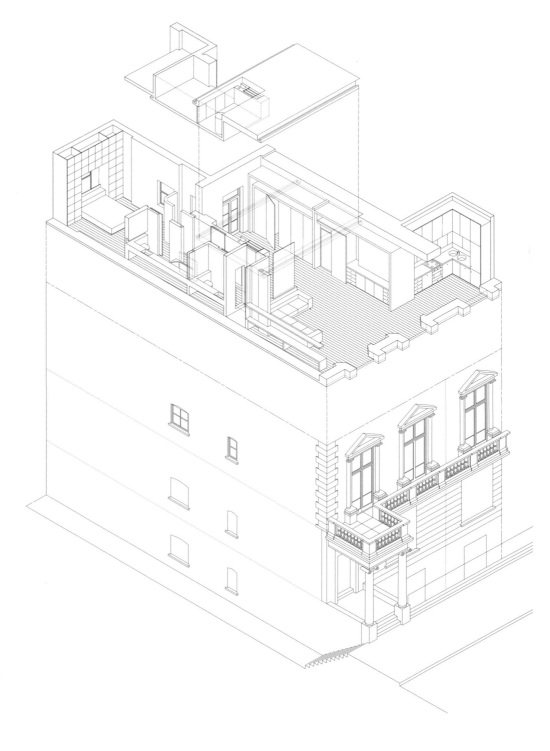

Above Right The isometric shows the partitions folded away. A new structural frame replaces bearing walls and supports the four-story structure above the apartment while allowing for an open plan. The living spaces retain the 3.6-meter (11.8-foot)-high ceilings; the bathrooms have a lower height to accommodate storage and utilities in the plenum above.

Above The etched-glass screen is one of many planar wall elements found throughout the apartment that define spatial boundaries. Here, it separates the more public areas in front and the bathrooms and bedroom toward the rear, without blocking the flow of light. The full-height glass wall that encloses the shower (seen on the right) brings natural illumination into the center of the apartment.

Roger Hirsch Architect with Myriam Corti, Home/Office for a Graphic Designer, New York, New York

This graphic designer's home doubles in function as an office that must accommodate two to three persons at work. This is achieved in a 600-square-foot (55.7-square-meter) area through a freestanding 13 × 8-foot (4 × 2.4-meter) cabinet that contains the office equipment and divides the space into living and sleeping quarters. The cabinet, constructed of plain-sliced maple veneer plywood in a satin finish, is the apartment's focal object and stands out in contrast with the white walls and the dark espresso-stained floor. When the doors are closed to use the space for living, the cabinet forms a lustrous wood partition whose cantilevered cushioned bench serves as both seating and guest bed.

Above The folding doors control the visual and literal clutter generated by the office—at the time that the space was designed, the owner's computer equipment was still large and cumbersome. They slide open on an overhead track and bottom wheels to reveal two full-sized workstations. The bench attached to the reverse side of the door conveniently disappears, while a magnet board folds back to reveal two openings that align with the window beyond to preserve the light and view. Since bifold doors of this size are not standard, the architects customized the design from various hardware components and had the metal track fabricated to accommodate the large panels. Yet even with these custom-made elements, the design remained budget conscious.

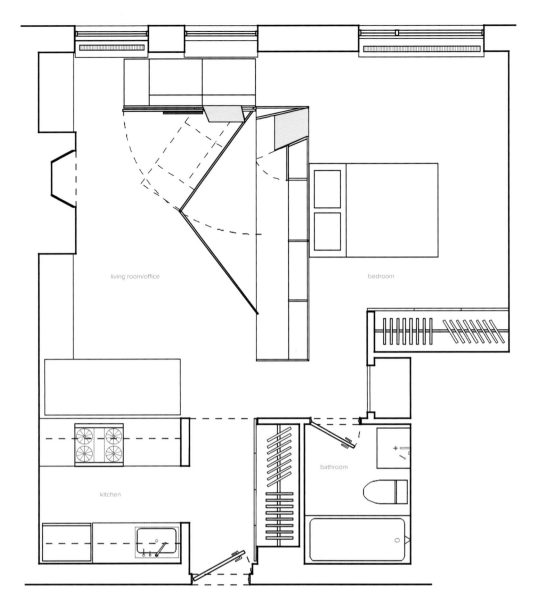

living room/office

bedroom

kitchen

bathroom

Above The project successfully separates home and office life by creating an either/or spatial condition, doubling function and space through compartmentalization. The dining table also serves as a work surface, when pushed toward the kitchen, gliding on wheels and along a channel hidden in the wall cabinet. The cabinet's inspiration was an engineering ruler: Transforming while unfolding, the wall of wood and metal emphasizes connections and precision throughout, contributing to a balanced and measured design.

Opposite On the bedroom side of the freestanding wall, the maple cabinet serves as a headboard and houses recessed night tables that fold down on both sides of the bed. The owner brings clients into the office area, but the cabinet is situated so as to block views into the bedroom. The small opening is angled to direct the eye toward the river vista outside. The straightforward, quiet architecture serves as a peaceful backdrop to the dual life played out each day in the space.

progression, ascent connection, revolutions, reach, movement, passage, sequence

Circulation

Kazuyo Sejima & Associates, Small House, Tokyo, Japan

Visible through the transparent rear façade of the structure, the spiral staircase within an open steel frame organizes and unifies the spaces of this house. Each floor was designed independently and stacked out of alignment with the one above or below it. The proximity of nearby buildings and the privileging of certain views and orientations determined these variations—a nimble solution to the puzzle of distributing the program vertically. The stair's placement within each space is thus deliberate: The design generates order from the interior core, an inversion of the typical urban building, where the interior is formed by the act of enclosure. Although the circulation core serves as the building's central spinal column, the delicacy of its elements makes it almost disappear at night.

Above The open steel shaft that surrounds the folded metal stair is painted white. The outer steel skeleton, a much more refined tubular structure, also white, supports the concrete floors at the perimeter. The exterior walls, which cant upward or downward at varying angles on each face of the room, echo the spiraling path through the house: Ascending or descending, the inhabitants experience a constantly changing environment.

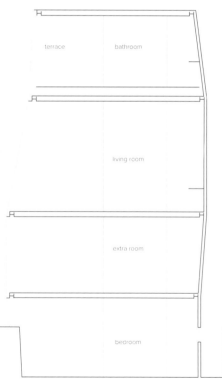

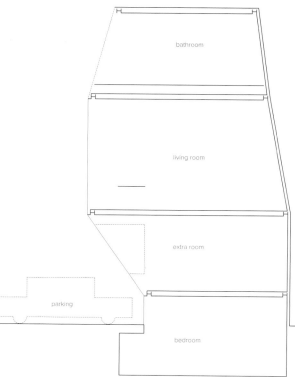

bathroom

living room

extra room

parking

bedroom

Above and Left Each level of this miniature tower for a couple with children is devoted to a different aspect of the program, and its size varies accordingly, with the main level, which accommodates the living, dining, and kitchen functions, given the greatest height and width. Throughout, the circulation and structure—almost pure geometric form—are exposed to the surrounding room to retain the clarity of the space.

noroof architects, Slot House, Brooklyn, New York

In this renovation of a row house, recurring compositional and material relationships form a coherent spatial experience. Although used as a bedroom, the ground floor has the stairwell as its central focus, which extends the vertical cut beyond the two main levels, downward to the cellar (accessed for the time being by a construction ladder) and upward to a new skylight. The architect-owners combined a preassembled galvanized metal stair with other off-the-shelf materials to create a layered composition. The circulation area serves also for storage: Hollow-core door panels mounted behind the stair conceal 1-foot (304.8-millimeter)-deep pull-out cedar drawers on one side and coat hooks on the other. On the lower landing, horizontal cedar boards hide a closet.

Above The second level, more spacious and light filled, serves as the living area. Here, the stairwell becomes not merely a connector but, rather, an architectural moment. The transparency of the metal grating that extends from the landing links the two levels visually and conceptually, adding to the richness of spatial layers.

Above Repeating the plywood of the stair-well door panels are the boxed-in joists of the skylight, whose opening is offset from that of the stair. The fenestration scheme not only brings sunlight into the stairwell and central living area, but also underscores the spatial idea of the slot.

Right Circulation runs along the vertical and horizontal axes, which intersect at the top landing of the stair. From within, the house reaches out toward the urban landscape and especially the 60-foot (18.3-meter)-tall maple in front, which the architects preserved and which, beloved by the neighborhood, implies community. In this way, the design crafts phenomenological character in the space while addressing practical concerns.

Opposite Their decision to preserve the magnificent maple in the deep front yard inspired the architects to cut a vertical opening in the façade to create views of the tree from within; this, in turn, led to the development of the slot as the primary spatial idea and organizer of the house. The flow of circulation can be glimpsed from the exterior façade, not just in what is seen through the windows but in the placement of the openings themselves. Movement is implied from the door to the large slotlike opening, extending the house both vertically and horizontally.

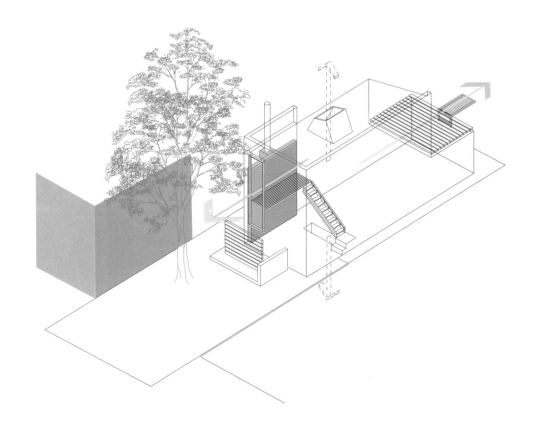

Cell Space Architects, Diagonal House, Tokyo, Japan

In the back corner of the house, the stair forms part of a composition of layers in various planes—including guardrail, shelving, wall, and window—that creates a sense of depth in a limited space. The translucent polycarbonate guardrail and slender steel profiles take on the tonal qualities and lightness of their surroundings. In its ephemerality, the stair disappears into the architecture. Moreover, because this corner sits opposite the room's wide glazed diagonal wall, the likely approach—oblique—would create a forced perspective were it not for the circulation. The stairwell removes tension from the corner, dissolving the angle through its slight structure and freeing the space to move upward.

Above Typically, the space under a stair, if used, is dedicated to closed storage. Here, however, it becomes open shelving sized to hold CDs and other objects. These shelves meld seamlessly into the stairwell, repeating its pattern from floor to ceiling, as well as recalling the horizontal striations from the diagonal façade outside. The underside of the stair is as finished as the top of the tread, the white surface creating a serene space of its own. The sculptural form of the stair continues the house's play of diagonals against rectilinear elements.

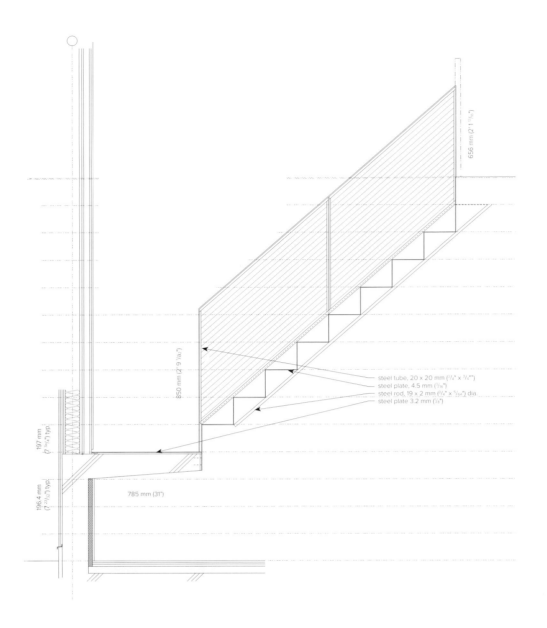

656 mm (2' 1 1⁄16")

850 mm (2' 9 3⁄32")

197 mm (7 3⁄4") typ.

196.4 mm (7 23⁄32") typ.

785 mm (31")

steel tube, 20 x 20 mm (3⁄4" x 3⁄4"")
steel plate, 4.5 mm (3⁄16")
steel rod, 19 x 2 mm (3⁄4" x 5⁄64") dia.
steel plate 3.2 mm (1⁄8")

Above The stair section is cut from the second landing to the second floor; the penultimate step is a winder that turns away from the elevation. The structure of slender rods and steel plates appears almost weightless. Two guardrail details are shown above the elevation.

Opposite A tall translucent window admits light into the back corner of the stairwell, which would otherwise be dim since almost all of the house's glazing occurs on its diagonal face. The tread side of the staircase and the landing are finished in a pale gray; the steel-plate landing aligns with the top of the bench and heating unit. The stair mediates opposing directions by forming a middle ground between the horizontal strata of the room, shelving, and bench and the verticality of the ladder of shelving against the full-height window. Rather than two planar systems, a complex space results. Artificial lighting for the stairwell is accordingly subtle and aligns with the shelving.

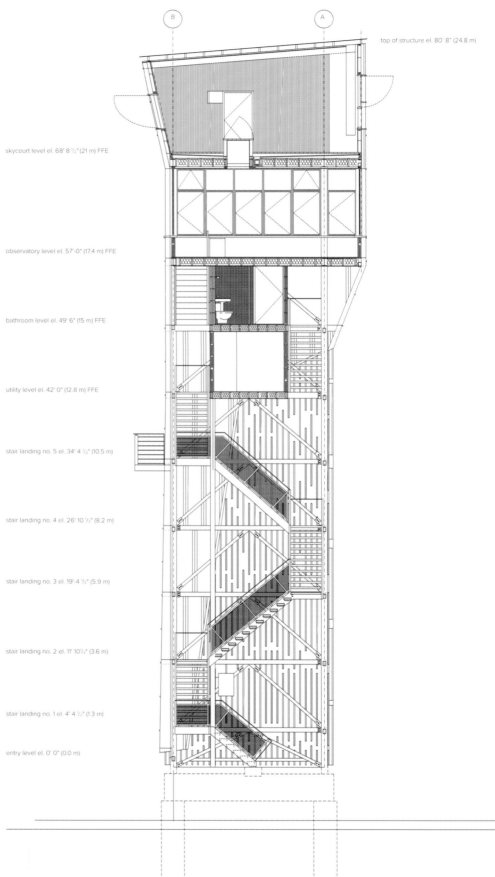

top of structure el. 80' 8" (24.8 m)

skycourt level el. 68' 8 ¹/₂" (21 m) FFE

observatory level el. 57'-0" (17.4 m) FFE

bathroom level el. 49' 6" (15 m) FFE

utility level el. 42' 0" (12.8 m) FFE

stair landing no. 5 el. 34' 4 ¹/₂" (10.5 m)

stair landing no. 4 el. 26' 10 ¹/₂" (8.2 m)

stair landing no. 3 el. 19'-4 ¹/₂" (5.9 m)

stair landing no. 2 el. 11' 10¹/₂" (3.6 m)

stair landing no. 1 el. 4' 4 ¹/₂" (1.3 m)

entry level el. 0' 0" (0.0 m)

Marlon Blackwell Architect, Keenan Tower House, Fayetteville, Arkansas

Corresponding with the tree canopy, the treetops, and the sky, the design for the tower house organizes its program into three main sections: the outdoor stair and utility rooms, the living area, and the skycourt. At the top, a fold-down stair provides access to the skycourt from inside the living and sleeping space.

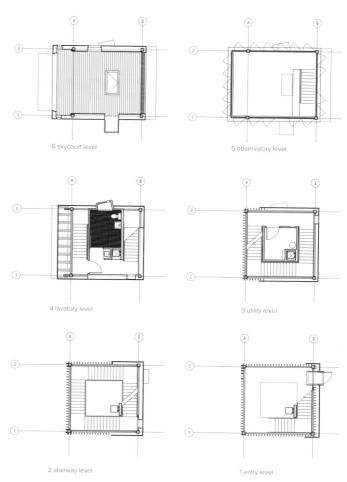

6 skycourt level

5 observatory level

4 lavatory level

3 utility level

2 stairway level

1 entry level

Above Left The entrance to the tower is through a deep metal portal on the metal-clad east façade. A bed of pecan shells on the forest floor leads to the base of the stair.

Above Right Each of the six levels, or zones, has a different degree of enclosure and openness to take advantage of particular vistas from the building. It takes about four revolutions to ascend to the observatory level.

Above Although the stair offers the only pedestrian access to the tower space above, it provides a pleasurable sequence of its own, with views of the hilly landscape that filter through the irregular rhythm of the oak fins. The lattice is held off on the square steel-tube frame.

Above A small vertical chase contains the utility lines for the residence and provides the structure for a dumbwaiter. The transparency of the metal grating against the brightness of the sky makes the stair read as an extension of the structural frame, so that the space feels unconstricted and airy.

Arakawa + Gins, Architectural Body Research Foundation, Reversible Destiny Lofts (In Memory of Helen Keller), Mitaka, Japan

The sloping floor planes and varying floor textures in these experimental apartments in a Tokyo suburb destabilize space physically and visually, prompting the inhabitants to reconsider their relationship with the environment. This procedural architecture represents a different sort of machine for living: The spatial environment invites what the architects hope to be "optimistic and constructive action" on the part of the inhabitants and provides them the opportunity to live extended lives, reversing the customary mortal decline, by stimulating their bodies and minds. The main living space has a floor like the surface of the moon, which leads one along a path of many unpredictable moments and details.

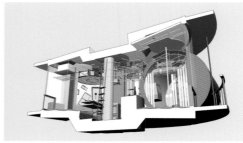

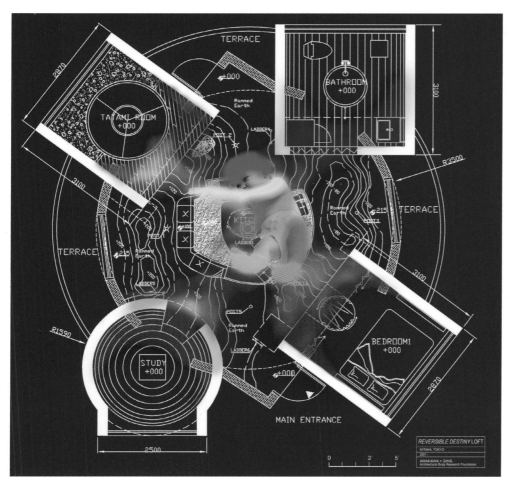

Above and Left Changes in elevation and the irregular terrain are keenly sensed, as shoes are not usually worn in the Japanese house. The varying topography of the interior, evident in the renderings, provides each room with a unique stimulating experience. Movement revolves around the centrally located sunken kitchen; centrifugal forces direct movement from this core into the three or four pods that serve as bedroom, bathroom, and study or meditation space. These pods intersect with the main space as distinct volumetric forms that give the interior an energetic aura.

Ordering of Contents

Rather than serving as an empty site in which loose furnishings are gathered, the house can integrate furniture into its architecture. In very small projects, though, the architecture can *be* the furniture, whether condensed into a single object, like the projects in "Capsules," or distributed as a system throughout the residence, like the projects in "Built-Ins and Convertibles." In practical terms, a streamlining of functions into compact forms, often concealed, preserves the openness of a dwelling. But by thinking at the scale of furniture and industrial design, designers have also forged a strong connection between architecture and human dimensions, bringing about a more intimate relationship between the object and the user. The projects collected here are defined by their emphasis on the functions of dwelling as opposed to function itself. Efficiency still remains a primary concern, whether people are housed or books are housed, and the mechanics of these systems are in fact clever. What matters, however, is that all of these projects devise a system of ordering contents to be imposed on the architectural elements.

The capsule may serve one or multiple functions, and it varies in dimension from an object within a larger space, as in the Caruso Apartment, to encompass the whole dwelling, in the case of the micro-compact home. The idea of the freestanding capsule evokes the monastic carrel in Antonello da Messina's 1475 painting *St. Jerome in His Study*, a favorite spatial exemplar for architects. The image frames the humanist saint working in a self-contained environment—a single piece of furniture incorporating table, bench, shelving, and walls—that is situated within a building whose windows open onto the landscape. Like the study depicted, the contemporary living module may serve as a place of shelter and retreat from the distractions of the larger world. Yet, despite the hermetic connotations of the term, these capsules do not turn inward: In the Caruso Apartment and the Home.in.1, the module constitutes a center into which and around which flows the life of the resident. The micro-compact home and the A-Z Cellular Compartment Unit both envision their modules as linked to an entire community. But the capsule does appear as a wish to simplify and pare down in its compressing of functions, which, in each of these projects, makes for an absolute immediacy between inhabitant and dwelling.

Built-in and convertible furnishings are considered here as pieces distributed throughout the space of the home and, in contrast to the capsules, are typically smaller individual pieces connected to the spatial envelope. Obviously, there is some overlap. The Future Shack straddles the categories and shares an affinity with the micro-compact home. The Fagelstraat Apartment is engaged with the exterior wall rather than freestanding but otherwise bears a resemblance to the "capsule" of the Caruso Apartment. The two-sided storage unit in the Ruth Avenue house is, like a capsule, virtually freestanding, yet it functions more like a built-in piece than an inhabitable volume.

The inhabitant of a 500-square-foot (46.5-square-meter) apartment does not necessarily have a proportionate fraction of the belongings of someone in a 2,000-square-
foot (186-square-meter) home. Possessions still need to be stowed somewhere, as
evidenced by the multitude of publications and television programs devoted to the art
of organization. Along with the practical end of keeping away clutter, built-in furniture provides a visually and psychologically more restful space. Whether as part of the
structure, like the sleeping platform and open shelves of Hut T, or as a fixed piece with
integrated functions, like the casework of Fagelstraat, compartmentalization makes
the world comprehensible by breaking down the functions of dwelling into the most
fundamental terms.

In the Loftcube, transformable elements take the form of double-sided "functional"
panels that can service either of two spaces and sliding panels that create flexible
spatial definition between demarcated areas. For a number of these projects, however,
the convertible pieces—folding up or down, sliding in or out—constitute a system of
appearing and disappearing objects within a neutral space. The single-room residences
of the Future Shack, the Hughston Studio, and the T.O. Penthouse take on the role of a
multipurpose living space, with none of the transparent markers of a bedroom, dining
room, or otherwise named space.

The projects collected in this section can be seen to offer opposing models of ordering objects and functions in a small space. On the one end, the A-Z Cellular Compartment Unit proposes a one-to-one relationship of function to space, forming artificial
boundaries to heighten awareness of individual activities. On the other, the T.O.
Penthouse resists typological categorization; it rethinks program as a series of events
taking place in a space whose identity is fluid. Architecture in the form of ordered
space provides a sense of control to the inhabitant. Whether it then imposes a regi-
men on the inhabitant or just provides a clean backdrop for a busy life depends on the
occupant.

cell, transportable,
array, self-contained,
cube, efficiency,
pixel, module,
condense

Capsules

Andrea Zittel, A-Z Cellular Compartment Unit, no fixed site

Intended to optimize the volume within a larger open space, the Cellular Compartment Unit is highly efficient, condensing programmatic elements into an array of equally sized blocks. This particular arrangement combines ten interconnected plywood-and-glass capsules banded by stainless steel edges; the possibilities for customizing the modules are, of course, infinite. Although rooted in the tendencies of the American home toward the compartmentalization of functions, the Cellular Compartment Unit compresses individual activities so intensely in space and time as to raise the inhabitants' awareness of how they engage each task or pastime.

Above Each 8 × 4 × 4-foot (2.4 × 1.2 × 1.2-meter) compartment is assigned an individual function, creating an instant order and efficiency to daily routines. The units hint at the possibility of organizing the inhabitant's way of life through an outward structuring of the dwelling. Although the compartments seem well suited for activities involving rest and work, no function is excluded, including those of the kitchen or bathroom. As with all her other dwellings, the artist inhabited one of the units as a "personal living experiment."

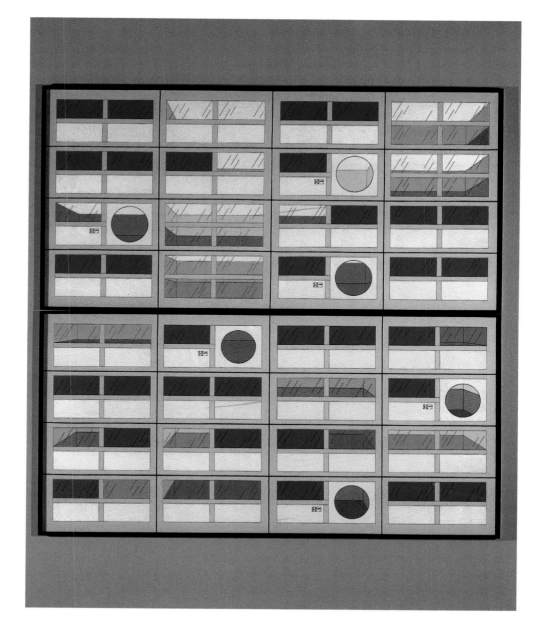

Above In Zittel's vision of entire communities of the modules, no space is privileged over another, which, together with the absence of separate circulation, suggests a further compacting of time, space, and function.

**Arts Corporation, Home.in.1,
no fixed site**

This project was commissioned as an interior renovation of sorts for a rented apartment. Because no structural interventions to the space were permitted, the module was designed to be freestanding and self-contained, ideally suited for the young client with a small budget living in an urban environment. The architect describes the 6-foot (1.8-meter) cubic module as a pixel: It forms a basic component but is suggestive of multiple units. The cube's contents leave a visible trace behind each of the twelve muted door panels. When the objects are backlit by the fluorescent tubes inside, the panels become a shadow theatre of light and color.

Above Each of the translucent acrylic doors swings open to reveal thick glass shelves that rest on a metal shelving system, used variously as bookcases, storage space, and a work station. Multiple casters provide mobility. The project blurs the boundaries between architecture, interior design, and furniture, a characteristic integration of scales and disciplines seen in the firm's work.

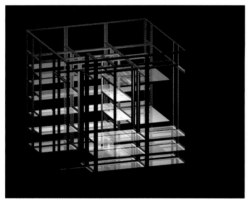

Above The project uses common, off-the-shelf materials chosen for their low cost and simplicity. Steel shelving angles, glass, and acrylic create an industrial aesthetic. The interchangeable pieces also make assembly and disassembly relatively simple for two people in two days.

Above Right The center of the cube is hollow for use as a walk-in closet. The Home. in.1 houses most of the owner's possessions, allowing for restful and orderly surroundings elsewhere in the apartment.

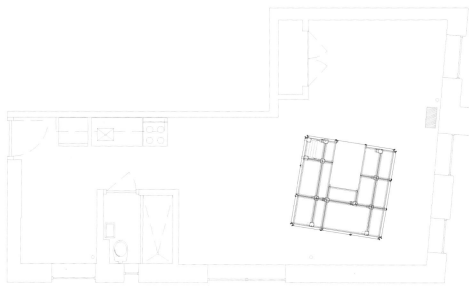

Above The work space is located on the opposite side of the closet. A power hub connected to the apartment brings electricity to the unit to provide artificial lighting on the interior and outlets at the workstation and nightstand. The front leg of a prefabricated aluminum ladder, hidden behind one of the doors, gives access to the sleeping platform above.

Left The original site of the Home.in.1 was a 700-square-foot (65-square-meter) apartment in New York City. Located centrally in the space, the cube made the apartment feel larger by concentrating most functions in one location. Since then, it has traveled to Las Vegas and Manila with the owner.

Dick van Gameren Architecten, Caruso Apartment, Amsterdam, Netherlands

The apartment is an updated unit inside a seventeenth-century warehouse. The environment is kept simple and finished in white to reflect light throughout. The design involved the removal of interior partition walls to free up the space, and the usual plan separations were instead pared down and centralized in a single object. The utility module occupies the center of the apartment and touches neither walls nor ceiling, allowing for an uninterrupted flow of space and daylight.

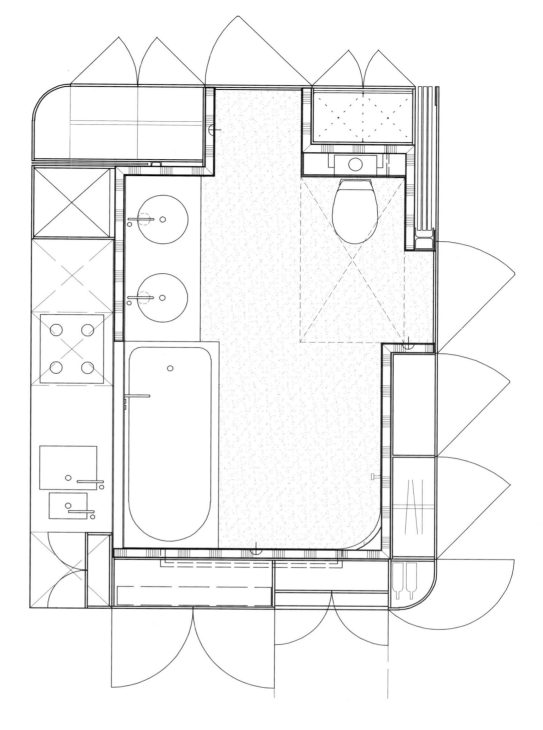

Above In addition to kitchen, bathroom, and storage, this compact volume conceals a dining table that folds down. Although the volume serves different functions on each side, a certain symmetry is kept in the form.

Above Sliding doors hung from an overhead track close off the bedroom from the rest of the space and are neatly stacked into a pocket in the capsule. Transparent panels at the ceiling give the bedroom additional privacy but maintain the free-floating appearance of the capsule.

Right and Opposite The efficient exterior of the volume belies its tranquil center. The bathroom is a space of relaxation, unusually spacious for a small apartment. The monochromatic palette of the mosaic tiles lends the module a monolithic, sculptural quality on the interior, as if it had been hollowed out of a block of ice. Located opposite an exterior window, the wall above the bathtub consists of two layers of sanded glass to admit diffuse light past the galley kitchen into the center of the volume. Clean, frameless connections inside and out give the volume a crispness and identity distinct from the surrounding space of the apartment.

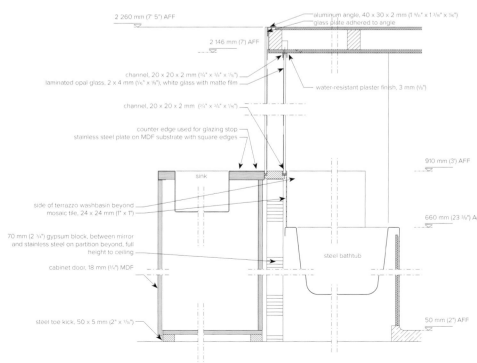

2 260 mm (7' 5") AFF

aluminum angle, 40 x 30 x 2 mm (1 9/16" x 1 3/16" x 1/16")
glass plate adhered to angle

2 146 mm (7') AFF

channel, 20 x 20 x 2 mm (3/4" x 3/4" x 1/16")
laminated opal glass, 2 x 4 mm (1/16" x 1/8"), white glass with matte film

water-resistant plaster finish, 3 mm (1/8")

channel, 20 x 20 x 2 mm (3/4" x 3/4" x 1/16")

counter edge used for glazing stop
stainless steel plate on MDF substrate with square edges

910 mm (3') AFF

sink

side of terrazzo washbasin beyond
mosaic tile, 24 x 24 mm (1" x 1")

660 mm (23 5/8") AFF

70 mm (2 3/4") gypsum block, between mirror
and stainless steel on partition beyond, full
height to ceiling

steel bathtub

cabinet door, 18 mm (3/4") MDF

steel toe kick, 50 x 5 mm (2" x 3/16")

50 mm (2") AFF

**Horden Cherry Lee and Lydia Haack +
John Höpfner Architekten, micro-compact
home (m-ch), no fixed site**

The micro-compact home, or m-ch, intends
to integrate manufacturing advances into
residential architecture. In its production
and upkeep, as much as its compactness, it
resembles a car: The factory customizes the
exterior color, provides replacement parts,
and recycles the unit at the end of its life. The
2.65-meter (8.7-foot) pod has an aluminum
rainscreen cladding and is fully insulated.
The lightweight structure may be delivered
by truck and craned into place or possibly
helicoptered to a site. Moreover, in many
localities, its small size frees the unit from
planning permits.

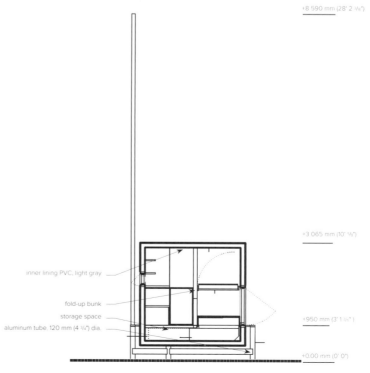

+8.590 mm (28' 2 3⁄8")

+3.065 mm (10' 3⁄8")

inner lining PVC, light gray

fold-up bunk

storage space

aluminum tube 120 mm (4 3⁄4") dia.

+950 mm (3' 1 3⁄8")

+0.00 mm (0' 0")

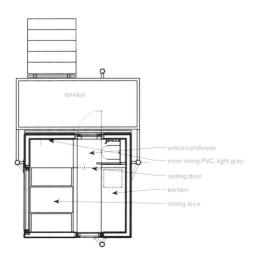

terrace

entrance/shower
inner lining PVC, light gray
sliding door
kitchen
dining area

Above and Left The units are intended as individual short-stay residences for business travelers or single holidayers or even as student housing; however, two units may be joined by adding a door at the end of the kitchen, thus accommodating two to four persons. The modularity of the capsules allows many potential groupings, including the vertical clusters proposed by the architects. Like a hotel or dormitory, all furnishings are integral to the unit.

Above The micro-compact home was inspired by the layered space and modular arrangement of the traditional Japanese teahouse. Half of the cube is dedicated to resting, eating, or working, and the other half to services. Each zone of the living unit contains two or more uses: For example, the entrance houses a shower and toilet, and the table in the sunken dining or work area may be stored to create more space for sleeping. The upper double bed–sized bunk can be folded up out of the way. Despite the diminutive volume and condensed functions of the pod, the inhabitant has the luxury of an outdoor terrace.

Above No additional furniture is required in the unit since everything, including stereo, plasma screen, communications systems, and utilities, is built in. Most of the furnishings are aluminum. Seven units were first introduced in the student village at the Technical University Munich, where the pods are arranged along an elevated walkway that supplies all utilities—electricity, water, and sewer.

integrated, unfolding, adaptability; stacking, duality, open plan, retractable, transformation, multipurpose

Built-Ins and Convertibles

Sean Godsell Architects, Future Shack, no fixed site

Designed as a shelter for all types of emergency and hardship situations, the Future Shack is trucked to its site and assembled in a little over a day's time from standardized components. While the exterior of this mass-produced residence is a weathered shipping container, the interior is lined with sheets of plywood.

Above and Above Right In the multipurpose room used for cooking, eating, and sleeping, perforated panels fold down from one side to serve as beds. When not in use, the beds and a table on the opposite side fit flush against the wall, revealing simple rectangular cutouts that function as pulls.

At the back, a white wall provides relief against the plywood surfaces. It conceals two doors: one opening on an alcove that contains a rudimentary kitchen, brightened by a splash of color on the interior wall; and another leading to the bathroom at the rear of the home. The minimalism of the space serves more than stylistic or orderly ends. It allows the components that make the unit functional and independent—water tanks, solar cell, satellite receiver, access ramp and ladder, and folding roof—to fit inside the container for shipping.

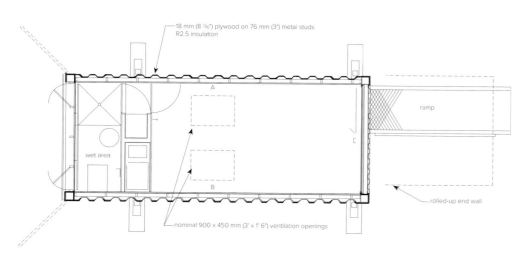

18 mm (8 ³/₁₆") plywood on 76 mm (3") metal studs
R2.5 insulation

A

ramp

wet area

B

rolled-up end wall

nominal 900 x 450 mm (3' x 1' 6") ventilation openings

Above and Left With the kitchen and bath—options that may be added to the unit depending on its application—the Future Shack becomes a self-contained habitat that requires no additional furnishings other than, perhaps, two chairs. Despite its intended use as temporary housing, the bathroom interior, featuring durable contemporary stainless steel fixtures, would not be out of place in a well-appointed urban home.

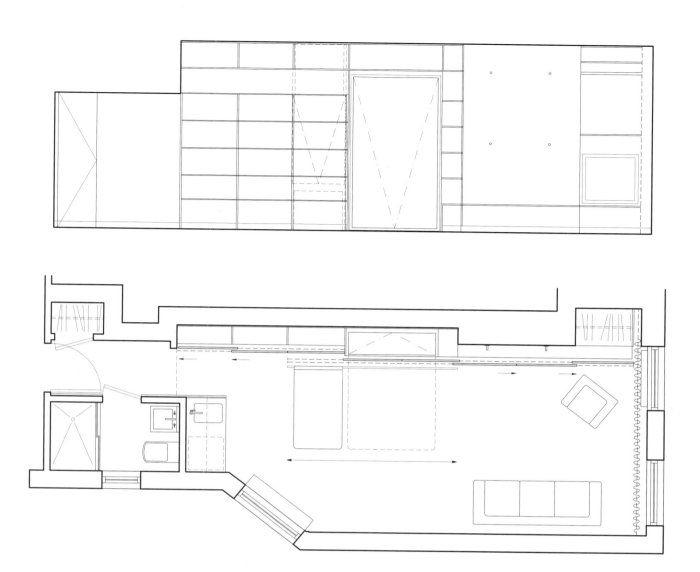

Joel Sanders Architect, Hughston Studio, New York, New York

The typical layout of the brownstone buildings of New York City is long and narrow with windows at each end. This studio apartment occupies one such space in Greenwich Village, a single room that assumes multiple activities—living, dining, sleeping, dressing, and storage—in 500 square feet (46.5 square meters). To optimize space, the architect devised a system of built-in furniture and storage along one wall of the studio, which frees up the room for a few additional pieces of seating. The curtain at the end of the room can be pushed into an alcove to vary daylighting conditions and to open up views of the rear garden.

Above The storage wall stretches across the width of the west elevation. Eight fabric panels, sliding on ceiling-mounted tracks, provide ease of access to the storage behind. Fabric was a more economical choice than custom millwork, and it achieves the same purpose, concealing a variety of household items under one consistent façade, with more striking results.

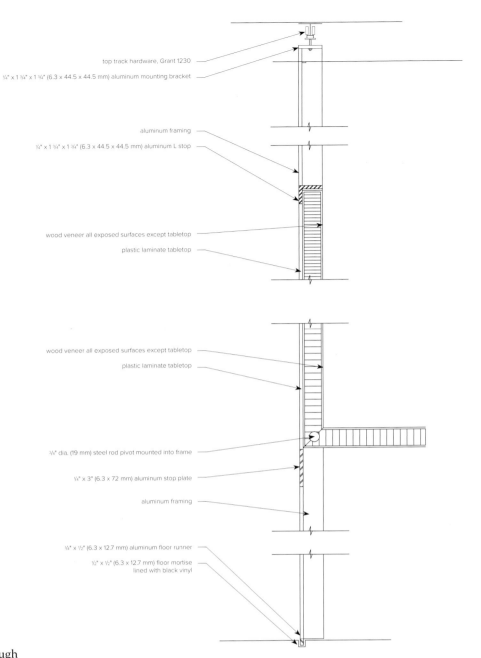

top track hardware, Grant 1230

¼" x 1 ¾" x 1 ¾" (6.3 x 44.5 x 44.5 mm) aluminum mounting bracket

aluminum framing

¼" x 1 ¾" x 1 ¾" (6.3 x 44.5 x 44.5 mm) aluminum L stop

wood veneer all exposed surfaces except tabletop

plastic laminate tabletop

wood veneer all exposed surfaces except tabletop

plastic laminate tabletop

¾" dia. (19 mm) steel rod pivot mounted into frame

¼" x 3" (6.3 x 72 mm) aluminum stop plate

aluminum framing

¼" x ½" (6.3 x 12.7 mm) aluminum floor runner

½" x ½" (6.3 x 12.7 mm) floor mortise lined with black vinyl

Above Right The kitchen has barely enough room for the sink and stove along one wall. The need for more counter space is solved with a fold-down table, moved to a position nearest the kitchen. The table, mounted to a frame that slides on short tracks attached to the floor and ceiling, can be relocated according to its service as a kitchen work surface, dining table, or desk.

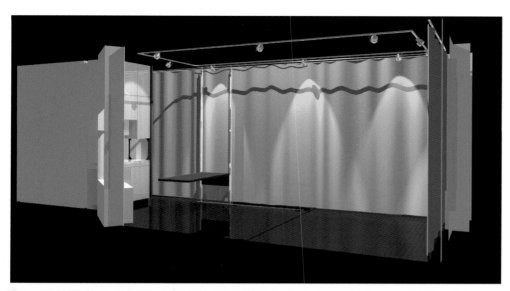

Above Left The L-shaped table is finished on one side in a mahogany veneer. In the upright position, the table panel creates a shallow shelf, also in mahogany. When pivoted down, the surface is a plastic laminate in a cheery turquoise hue. Adjacent shelving behind the curtain stores kitchenware. The fabric panels part in the evening to reveal a Murphy bed within a mahogany-lined alcove in the storage wall. The recess also contains a nightstand, shelving, and a reading light.

Pool Architektur, T.O. Penthouse, Vienna, Austria

This studio apartment is transformed when the furnishings are rolled out from the wall. What appears to be a dark gap around the headboard of the bed is actually the profile of a table that extends into the same zone. When not in use, bed, table, and adjacent storage closet neatly disappear, leaving a painted panel flush with the wall.

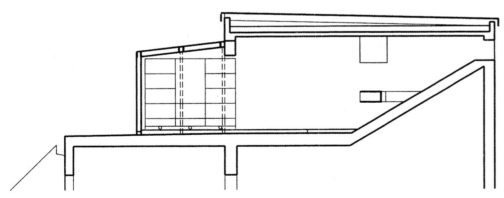

Above The storage closet provides more than enough space for clothes and other household items. The penthouse contains no other cabinetry: Such a large volume of storage would take up too much space were it not a mobile piece.

Left The penthouse occupies the space of a former water tank on the roof of an industrial building. Due to existing structural load limitations, the only addition has been the enclosure for the roll-away pieces, which forms a small protrusion beyond the main volume.

Above The kitchen's unusual configuration, with a refrigerator mounted to the ceiling and a steel counter attached to the inclined wall, makes use of an awkward space created by the stairwell to the penthouse. A single wall-mounted sink serves as kitchen sink and bathroom lavatory and shares a space with the shower. Further evidence of flexible use is a television located on a turntable drum built into the far wall, for viewing in both the living room and the toilet on the other side.

Right The built-in pieces occupy otherwise unusable space on the rooftop, keeping partitions and fittings to a minimum in the interior.

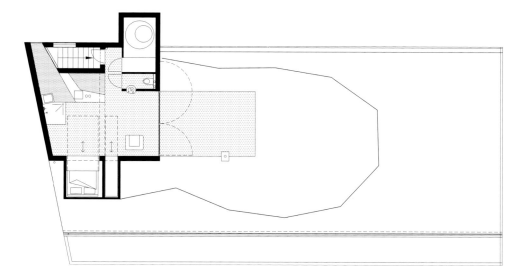

Above The penthouse itself consists of only 18 square meters (193.7 square feet). But the outdoor terrace, which continues the concrete floor past a frameless opening the width and height of the room, almost doubles the living space. Two wide glass doors swing outward for panoramic views of the Vienna rooftops.

Studio Aisslinger, Loftcube, no fixed site

Just as the exterior walls of this nomadic
rooftop residence can be customized to suit
the personal taste of the occupant, fixed and
sliding panels (both opaque and translucent)
create flexible and individualized spatial
definition between living and sleeping areas,
kitchen and bathroom.

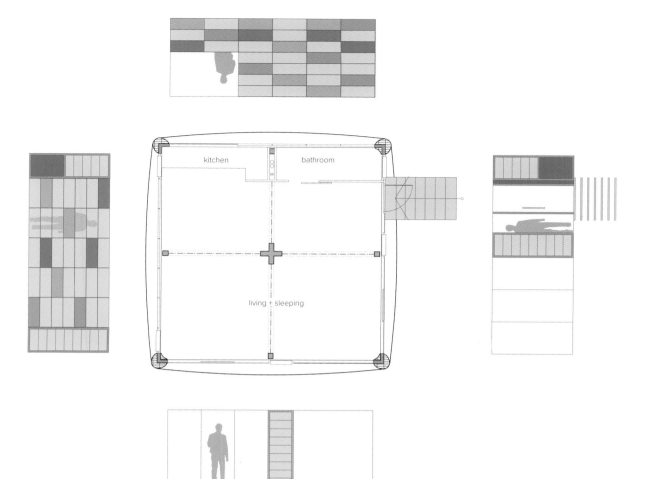

kitchen

bathroom

living + sleeping

Above The 6.6 × 6.6 meter (21.7 × 21.7 foot) modular frame is sufficiently compact to preclude the use of expensive steel members and to allow for an open plan inside. The double-sided panels on tracks create the basic living partitions, onto which all portable furniture modules affix themselves.

Above Two double-sided functional panels, which are fabricated from thermoformed white polystyrene, integrate plumbing into their cores. One of these panels contains a showerhead that flips from one side to the other for either showering in the bathroom or watering plants in the living area.

Above The functional wall panel between kitchen and bathroom features a faucet that extrudes seamlessly from either side to serve both the kitchen sink and the washbasin. The flexibility of these elements eliminates the need for duplicated fixtures; this clever multileveled minimalism makes the space efficient without any feeling of want or meagerness.

Maier + Zelter, Ruth Avenue, Austin, Texas

A double-sided storage cabinet divides this duplex into an open living space and smaller spaces for sleeping, bathing, and cooking. The storage wall has a strong presence as an architectural element, yet it retains the feel of a piece of furniture: discretely articulated, with vibrant panels framed by a thick white oak band on three sides. The block directly serves three spaces—living room, bedroom, and hallway—and contains a home office workstation. The change from the disengaged yellow-green block to the full-height red panels marks the more intimate, private space of the bedroom.

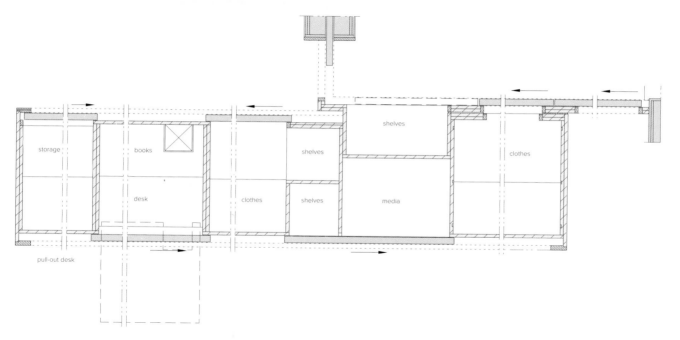

storage

books

desk

clothes

shelves

shelves

shelves

media

clothes

pull-out desk

Above and Left A series of planes close off the bedroom from the rest of the house. Two act as sliding doors for the storage cabinet and are also visible from the living room side. The skylight above the hallway leading to the bedroom also houses the pull-down ladder to the attic. The ladder has a finished frame on the ceiling side and thus appears as a roof window.

i29 Office for Spatial Design, Fagelstraat Apartment, Amsterdam, Netherlands

Attached to one wall of this renovated apartment, a compact millwork box encloses the bathroom, kitchen, and storage. By consolidating these functions, the remaining space reads as a continuous whole. The custom-designed assembly organizes the public area into separate zones, with dining and communal space in the kitchen at the front of the apartment and a more restful living room behind.

Left The omission of pulls on the doors and cabinet fronts contributes to the expression of the volume as an autonomous object. The architects consider the cabinet to be the heart of the home around which everything revolves, a *leefmachine* or "living machine."

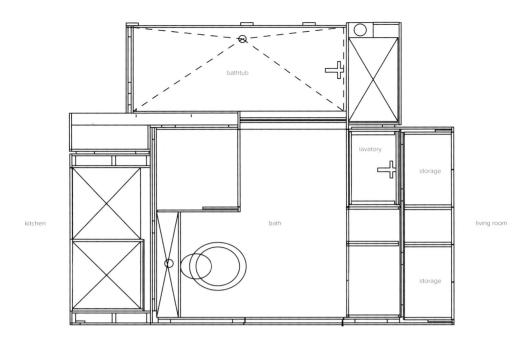

Above and Right The built-in unit covers the irregular walls of the apartment. Rather than a room with drywall partitions, it is a meticulously constructed piece of millwork, made of MDF sprayed to a glossy white finish and bamboo veneer plywood.

bathtub

lavatory

storage

kitchen

bath

living room

storage

MDF with spray-painted finish and bamboo plywood

plywood cabinets with polyester finish

epoxy coating at other room surfaces

Above The interior of the bathroom bursts with intense color, in sharp contrast with the mostly white palette of the apartment. Storage, fixtures, and walls are integrated, and with the walls, ceiling, and floor all finished in the same glossy green, the space eliminates the hierarchical order of surfaces to feel more like the inside of a cabinet. Only the faucet indicates that the alcove is really a lavatory.

Kazunari Sakamoto Architectural Laboratory, Hut T, Minamitsuru-gun, Yamanashi Prefecture, Japan

The coherence of materials—wood and plywood are used for nearly all surfaces—lends the house an informal, cabinlike feel, which suits its use as a weekend residence. The table in the foreground may be folded away to devote the space to the performance of chamber music. Since the house is not occupied on a daily basis, the problem of concealing large amounts of domestic effects is not an issue. Instead, the architecture imparts "diffusion and release," with everything placed out in the open.

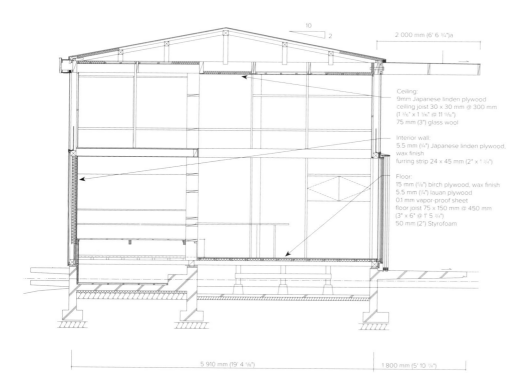

Ceiling:
9mm Japanese linden plywood
ceiling joist 30 x 30 mm @ 300 mm
(1 ³⁄₁₆" x 1 ³⁄₁₆" @ 11 ¹³⁄₁₆")
75 mm (3") glass wool

Interior wall:
5.5 mm (¼") Japanese linden plywood,
wax finish
furring strip 24 x 45 mm (2" x 1 ³⁄₄")

Floor:
15 mm (⁵⁄₈") birch plywood, wax finish
5.5 mm (¼") lauan plywood
0.1 mm vapor-proof sheet
floor joist 75 x 150 mm @ 450 mm
(3" x 6" @ 1' 5 ¾")
50 mm (2") Styrofoam

10
2

2 000 mm (6' 6 ¾")a

5 910 mm (19' 4 ⁵⁄₈")

1 800 mm (5' 10 ⁷⁄₈")

Above The interior wood frame is an extension of the open wood grid of the structural system and serves to organize the interior space without solid partitions. The layering of wood elements imbues the structure with abstractness: The furnishings become planes, while the space becomes an open lattice. The built-in components, like the mezzanine that serves as a sleeping platform, are not separate solids but integral to the structure, resulting in spaces that overlap and interpenetrate. As a result, views through the house provide a great degree of literal and implied transparency.

Left The geometry of the wood frame and largely glazed exterior continues in the interior. The Hut T plays with three different scales of space, with the lowest height at the mezzanine level. The light wood construction suits this small-scale house—which can in fact accommodate ten people—near Lake Yamanaka and Mount Fuji.

Surfaces and Finishes

Surface treatments differentiate spaces, call attention to details, interact with lighting, and complement or contrast with the surrounding environment. Designers are often reluctant to use strong palettes or patterns in a small space, for fear of oversaturated color or overscaled form. The projects collected here reveal that the inventive application of hues and textures greatly enriches the small dwelling. Whether used sparingly but with adequate punch or deeply layered, the hues and textures throughout these projects, varying in intensity from one surface to another, from one space to the next, convey an attitude toward the architecture that is not merely ornamental.

Color creates atmosphere: Certain hues register particular tonalities and values, such as warm or cool, vibrant or muted. The projects in "Hues" offer a sweep of possibilities. The cacophony of saturated pigments in the Reversible Destiny Lofts, the unexpected pop of blue and red in the Lignano Studio, and the overlapping wash of light-generated hues in the Young House demonstrate how vibrant colors can deepen the spatial experience. The monochromatic Chelsea Apartment, the pale gray and white of the Fold House, and the mostly white Natural Illuminance House show how even muted schemes develop the architectural idea. Of course, different values are often juxtaposed in the same space. Both the Fold and Natural Illuminance Houses reveal sudden moments of intense color. In the Flat in Little Venice the subdued kitchen front frames a lively band of multihued shades.

These projects use color spatially and architecturally, in ways that defy boundaries. To stimulate the senses, in the Reversible Destiny Lofts every conceivable surface, without regard to type, is highly and seemingly randomly colored. To highlight the sculptural quality of forms in the Chelsea Apartment, the muted green of the ceiling flows like a waterfall down the rear wall. To define a zone of activity, the bright blue hue of the Lignano Studio overruns borders of walls, floor, and ceiling. To create a focal point, the Little Venice flat treats its kitchen cabinets as the raw canvas for a color-field painting.

In some of these works, applied pigment is secondary to external conditions that bring color to the project. The Fold House uses the gray/white of its interior/exterior planes to draw on shifts in levels of daylight so that its surfaces absorb the changing hues of the sky. In the Natural Illuminance House, the frugal appearance of a painted hue is set against grids of filtered daylight and the glow of light from below. For both, minimal use of pigmented color reinforces the simplicity and luminosity of the architectural setting. In the Young House, color is purely derived from light. The mutable hues of the lights—which can be altered at will—create the illusion of planes that recede or advance in space.

The environments in "Textures" amplify architectural form through the use of textured materials. Texture, like color, communicates design intent through the associations generated by certain materials, which can imply a whole range of temperatures and related emotional responses. The rich cedar siding of the Canyon View Office and Guesthouse blends in with the wooded lot, but it also suggests a warmth in contrast to the sharply angled planes of the structure that might be of comfort to the psychologist's clients. At 15 Clifton Street, weathered wood is paired with oxidized Cor-Ten steel, tempering the industrial effect. Here, too, the integral color of the Cor-Ten plays off of the deep shadows carved out by the corrugated surface.

Tactility adds depth to a surface, which then becomes more animated. In a small home, this quality can vary the experience of a single space. Since the surface characteristic of an object—glossy, dull, fuzzy, coarse—can change the way that light is reflected on it and within the space in general, lighting design significantly affects texture. In the Hughston Studio, the track lighting helps to contrast the textures of the Teflon-coated fabric panels and the rough brick wall on opposite sides of the room; the sheen of the metallic-weave window curtain and the ebony-stained floor add a luxurious note. Texture may also take the form of visual pattern. By breaking up planes, pattern may change the perception of space. In this regard, it becomes a functional tool, disrupting the form of small boxy rooms or masking irregularities and imperfections in a surface. The bold graphics of the wallpaper in the study of the Echo Park House add dimension even when viewed from outside. Texture can create spatial complexity, without relying on interior objects such as furniture or decorative items. In the Slot House, the finishes are no afterthought. The discovery of a brick wall early in the renovation generated as many ideas about texture as about form. The result throughout is a rich overlay of smooth and rough surfaces, both among wood finishes and in contrast to the varying steel grids.

Contemporary design has often shied away from the use of bold finishes—consider the modernist buildings of the New York Five, otherwise known as the Whites—due to a focus on the manipulation of pure form and space. In some circumstances, this is appropriate. Even so, the concept behind the design may be deepened as finishes, even if additive in the form of textiles and pigment, bring another layer of complexity to the architecture. Hues and textures engage the inhabitant in a sensory rather than cerebral way, and they can evoke an emotional response. Perhaps the clearest example of this multivalency is found in the Young House: Already a sublime space in its monochromatic manifestation, the project becomes more emphatic and compelling, despite the increased abstraction of forms, once it is flooded with color.

value, pigment, gradation, intensity, blending, saturation, monochromatic, tone, luminosity

Hues

**Arakawa + Gins, Architectural Body
Research Foundation, Reversible Destiny
Lofts (In Memory of Helen Keller),
Mitaka, Japan**

Varying combinations of the three geometric forms—sphere, cube, and cylinder—are stacked like brightly colored building blocks in this complex of nine lofts. The exterior and interior are equally highly pigmented, unusual in most multiunit dwellings. For this controversial project, the saturation of color advances the same purpose as the destabilization of architectural form and surface: to provoke and excite the senses, not unlike an intense form of environmental psychology. Through these spaces, the artist-designers probe scientific theories that connect enhanced motor coordination to increased neural activity as well as the philosophical relationship between the mind and body.

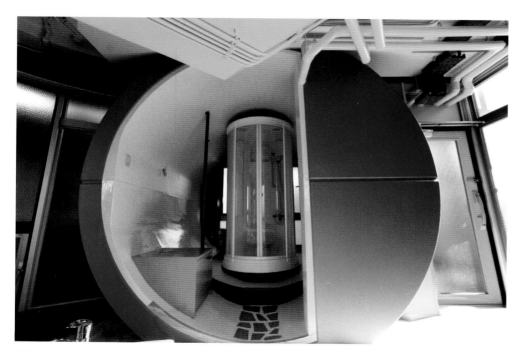

Above Nowhere in these lofts does color carry programmatic connotations, nor does it serve as a projection of an ideal sense of being in the inhabitants, as it would in many homes. Nevertheless, color is in fact a program: Just as the designers equip the lofts with directions for use, the predetermined hues serve an edifying purpose.

Top Left A complementary scheme juxtaposes saturated colors in this particular loft. Fourteen hues are incorporated throughout the entire complex. Color is used whimsically, so that the space appears as cheerful as a child's playroom. Each surface and individual element is articulated with a different hue, which generates a dynamism of objects that provides the eye with constant stimulus.

**Dennis Wedlick Architect,
Chelsea Apartment, New York, New York**

A muted paint scheme accentuates the architectural form of the main living space in the apartment. The rectangular room is kept open, but the treatment of the ceiling and wall planes, inspired by the idea of a proscenium, organizes the space into zones. Each of the architectural elements is assigned a subtly dissimilar hue within a limited range of greens and browns from Benjamin Moore: The soffits are Manchester Tan, the outer walls are White Dove, and the ceiling is Hancock Green. As the rear wall curves down from above, its green hue makes it seem an extension of the ceiling.

Above The crisp geometry of the kitchen contrasts with the curved forms of the outer room but exudes the same sense of streamlined cleanliness. The deep smoky-gray glass tile in a white grid of grout creates depth in the space, and although the color is dark, it is in the same tonal family as the pale hues on the walls. Cabinets, counter, and integral sink are all monochromatic to blend with the walls, while the absence of pulls (other than on appliances) provides a seamless appearance.

Right According to the designer, spectrally complex paint colors achieve an effect akin to the use of flip paint on a car: These colors vary when seen from different angles and in changing lighting conditions, an effect that enhances the sculptural form of the architecture.

Above The use of 3-inch (76-millimeter) rounded corner bead grants the walls more volumetric form and softer shadings of color. While most vertical edges are rounded, horizontal edges are squared. Adjustable recessed lighting highlights the rounded corners and enhances the tonal shifts.

**LOT-EK, Lignano Studio,
New York, New York**

Color here defies the customary divisions of planes into wall, floor, and ceiling. The bright blue envelopes a zone for architectural intervention and defines a realm of its own. In a space this small—the entire studio is a mere 485 square feet (45 square meters)—the usual planar separations would only reinforce the boundaries of the room. The witty and vivid color scheme has a pop clarity, proving that bold forms and colors do not necessarily overwhelm a small space.

Opposite The closet alcove contains storage and hides the top half of the graphic-covered bed; the bottom half serves as a continuation of the apartment's seating. The blue paint—Benjamin Moore's Utah Sky—infiltrates the alcove as well and makes it an extension of the room's volume.

Above Cutouts in the wall between kitchen and dining area give the impression that the stainless steel counter flows into the larger space as a dining table. Blue strips bracket the location of the table above and below: It is clearest here how the blue paint projects the plan of the apartment onto the floor and ceiling.

Above The small window behind the work space is fitted with a sheet of two-sided reflective Mylar, framing either the furnishings and art on the opposite side of the room or, when lit, the interior of the bathroom on other side of the wall. Deep red objects pepper the space against the blue field, from the towel and toiletry labels seen through the bathroom window to the cord ties on the telephone (as well as the light fixtures, toaster, and artwork elsewhere). These small details shift the perception of everyday objects and create coherence out of multiple forms in limited space.

Left The blue painting scheme also serves to mask the irregular structure of boxed-out beams and columns or chases on the walls and ceiling. Reminiscent of plumb-line markings on a construction site, red and graphite lines mark off a regular grid on the bare plaster walls and ceiling between the borders of blue paint. The two surface treatments combine the roughness of raw space with finished precision.

Jonathan Clark Architects, Flat in Little Venice, London, United Kingdom

A vibrant multihued band of color runs in an irregular rhythm across the wall cabinets of a kitchen in central London. The panels, which resemble a color-field painting, were custom painted by the artist Richard Clark to reflect the hues in a large screen print of a film poster for *Blow Up* hung in the adjacent living area. Though the surrounding olive-drab cabinets and stainless steel countertops are physically more forward, their subdued tones recede in contrast to the lively color in the center.

Above The kitchen occupies a full wall at one end of the open-plan living space. The walls and furnishings in the apartment vary from white to brown in color; thus the abstract band stands out. The white reveal of the wall that surrounds the block of cabinets gives the unit lightness, so that it does not overwhelm the space. Cove lighting at the ceiling sustains this impression. The monotone cabinets form a neutral and uniform frame for the colorful composition recessed within. A small window punctuates the wall with a bright flash of daylight, dissolving form around it. Ghostly spots of color appear behind the etched-glass backsplash, which continues over the lower half of the window well.

**Cell Space Architects, Fold House,
Nagareyama, Chiba, Japan**

The space of the house develops from a
sectional idea of the layering, wrapping, and
sliding of ribbed sheets that become the
building envelope. The ribbon of metal gives
the house its angled form, creating sheltered
outdoor spaces and eaves. The exterior surface is painted white to reflect sunlight and
decrease the thermal load on the building.
The absence of color also makes the building
reflective of changing weather and lighting
conditions.

Above and Left The dominant color effect varies in the course of a day. In the evening, the white interior is illuminated while the outer surfaces takes on the color of the dusky sky, but during the day, the structure presents a strong form with its planes of white and gray. On a clear day, the blue-gray inner surface of the shell blends with the color of the sky—rarely a true blue in Tokyo. The folds and cuts in the surface create abstract wedges of subtle color.

Above At one end of the house, hidden within the pallid gray-and-white fazolds, is the highly saturated color of the bathrooms. Because these rooms constitute enclosed spaces separate from the open areas of the house, the intense color comes as a surprise. A carmine-red angle is further splintered by its reflection in a vanity and its continuation in an intersecting shelf.

Above Here, the brilliant red and aubergine paint applied to the wedges that result from the folding manipulations create floating forms of color. Even the smallest odd-shaped spaces do not shy away from bold hues; rather, this approach reinforces the quirky geometry of the building.

Endoh Design House with Masahiro Ikeda, Natural Illuminance House, Tokyo, Japan

In this mostly white building, the black surfaces—both floor and ceiling—of the service area emphasize the verticality of the space and its interpretation as a single void. The black tile and gray grout reiterate the idea of the grid at a smaller scale. Color is used to differentiate other spaces from the primary volumes constructed from the serene white square grid.

Above and Left At the entrance to the bedroom level, one red door leads to the toilet enclosure, and another red door opens onto the bathing area. The light emanating from the basement level comes from the fluorescents used to illuminate the storage area. This artificial lighting can be varied so that, glowing through the grating, it imparts a cool or warm tint to the otherwise white room.

**tonkin liu, Young House,
London, United Kingdom**

Rather than a fixed paint scheme, this house has available the full spectrum of color. Adjusted by a computer-controlled lighting system, color-changing neon bulbs, hidden in coves and soffits throughout, constantly shift perceptions of the space. During the daytime, with the lights turned off, the house reveals a sleek and monochromatic interior. While the room is free of color, the quiet, austere forms may be enjoyed for their clean-edged simplicity, but this quality of the architecture is also what creates the impression of glowing volumes, solids, and planes of color in the evening. The white surfaces of the furniture and three interior towers serve as a canvas onto which color is projected. The floors and ceilings, a gloss resin, follow three gradations of hue from blue at the lower level to white in living room at the top. On the ground level, in the blue-lit kitchen, white glazed windows resemble giant light boxes.

Opposite With the stair illuminated in orange and the space beyond in green, the forms of the staircase become less apparent and the volume more so. The owner, a high-tech consultant, was captivated by a James Turrell light sculpture, which became the inspiration for the design of the house. As in the artist's work, light creates an ambiguity in the house between form and surface.

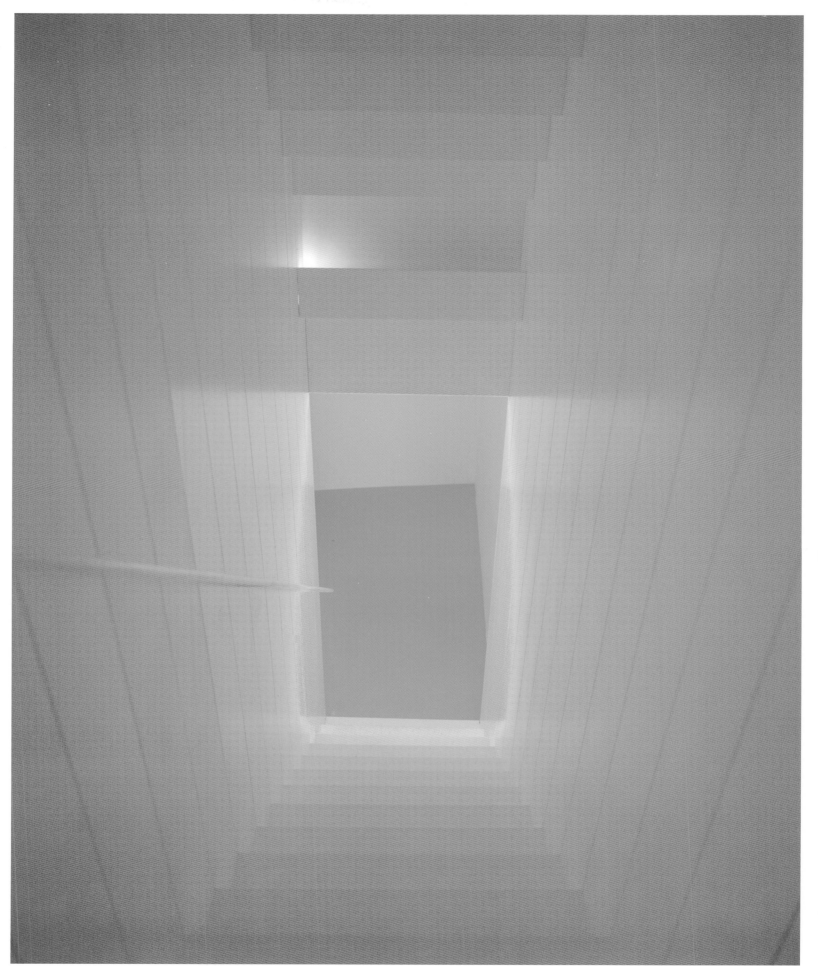

Above Instead of the pallid or yellowish cast of typical fluorescent and incandescent light, upbeat color fills the house. The light is directed precisely so that color can envelop very specific surfaces or flood and blend with another color. Each tower element (for sleeping, ambulating, cooking/washing) can take on a different color. The yellow-green translucent panel, which conceals the shower, glows as an entire illuminated wall.

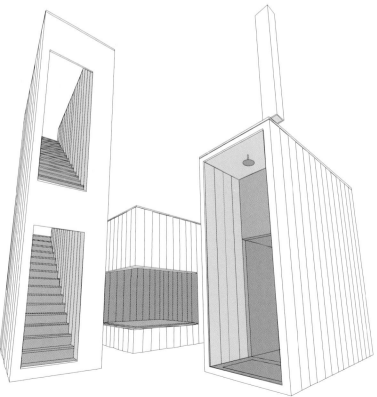

Above The white rectangle of light behind the bed is an illuminated alcove rather than the projection it seems, and it serves as both nightstand and reading light. The indirect and hidden light sources free the spaces of harsh shadows.

Left The small house consists of a single open space (except the enclosed bath) on each floor, but cutouts in the floor and the three vertical elements link the three levels. The small open plan of the house forms an advantage in the application of this lighting and color idea, as the effect would be lost in isolated rooms. Color flows freely between levels, with unbroken views of contrasting and blending light.

surface, oxidation, coating, weave, feel, materiality, nap, striation, grain, tactility

Texture

Uni Architects, 15 Clifton Street, Cambridge, Massachusetts

Light grazing the russet surface of the corrugated Cor-Ten steel emphasizes its coarse grain. The oxidized surface forms a protective coating on the steel, used here as an exterior cladding on the sides and roof of the house.

Above The small gable-end house is typical of the neighborhood. Despite its strong coloring, the house retains a contextual identity, as the ridged texture of the steel seems in place with the wood and foliage of the neighborhood. The flat, clean façade forms a striking contrast with the organic imperfections of the roof and sides, where the rust has run off onto the foundation.

Opposite The palette of dissimilar materials—Cor-Ten walls, concrete foundation, gravel driveway, the addition's vertical wood siding, and bamboo plantings—conveys tranquility with similarly scaled textures and simple forms.

**Kanner Architects, Canyon View Office/
Guesthouse, Los Angeles, California**

A psychologist's home office and guesthouse
appears as one unfolding ribbon of wood;
the horizontal striations of the cedar siding
contribute to the ambiguity of the form.
The carefully mitered acute angles become
seamless, and a few vertical joints control the
length of the boards that otherwise appear
continuous.

Above The wood windows, with their slender
frames, add to the consistency of the surface.
Although the materials are homogeneous
and the surfaces planar, the grain and color of
the cedar boards vary sufficiently to give the
wall a dynamic, shifting quality.

Above Angular forms abound between the smooth wood building and the irregular textures of the broken concrete steps and retaining walls, liriope beds and bamboo hedges. The sharpness of the whole suits the steep slope of the site.

Opposite The emphasis on surface is reinforced by the fenestration and openings in the walls that seem like incisions in the wood planes. The lushly vegetated site pervades the experience of the structure: Every view juxtaposes the complementary textures of building and foliage.

**Noroof Architects, Slot House,
Brooklyn, New York**

The house builds up a vocabulary of materials and compositional forms from one space to another, which provides an accretive reading of the building. Subtle repetition of square and right-angled elements in different materials and at different scales creates architectural motifs that impart coherence to the varied textures throughout. A shift from smooth to rough wood surfaces unifies the horizontal and vertical elements. The warmer tones of the irregular wood surfaces balance the colder precision of the three types of steel gratings.

Above The three steel gratings are seen layered through space. The grids of varying dimensions and shapes filter the view of the living space above. Ovals in the stair treads alleviate the severity of the rectilinear forms. Other steel grids continue outside the house in the form of a deck guardrail created from the metal mesh used for lobster traps and a cantilevered steel table on the deck.

Above Cedar boards appear again at the front entrance to the house. The new brick-and-wood elements recall the original structure of the house, a timber-and-brick infill wall that the architects left exposed and that adjoins the glazed slot opening. The house incorporates cement Hardiplank fiberboard and vinyl siding on the exterior. The choice of vinyl was both contextual and cost based; however, the vinyl strips avoid the imitation wood-grain texture of most synthetic sidings.

Above The right-angled ladder motif is found in the pull-out storage system behind the stair, which juxtaposes the smooth blackened-steel handle with the raw rotary-cut grain of the cedar boards.

**Joel Sanders Architect, Hughston Studio,
New York, New York**

Diverse surface finishes in the studio apartment reflect light in numerous ways, lending richness to a small volume. The room is a thorough study in tactility, with each side of the room given a different treatment: The smooth reflective finish on the dark-stained wood floor provides depth without absorbing excessive light, the gold Teflon-treated fabric panels are tailored but hang gently, while the semiopaque curtain that covers the brick end wall has a metallic shimmer. An exposed brick wall across from the storage wall provides a more informal dimension.

Above and Left The use of several deep hues in a single room creates impact through a combination of both matte and burnished surfaces; the wide range of textures is united through the limited color families. The nonreflective surfaces of the upholstery and linens, such as the thick woven bedcover that creates a chiaroscuro effect, recede against the lustrous gold panels and mahogany in the alcove and side table. The orientation of the mahogany grain—horizontal above the bed and vertical in the side table—accentuates the breadth rather than height of the alcove.

Barbara Bestor Architecture, Echo Park House, Los Angeles, California

The bold red-and-white wallpaper, custom-designed for the architect by the graphic artist Geoff McFetridge, frames a view of the greenery outside the study. (Bestor has also designed wallpapers with animated two-tone graphics derived from the patterns of moss, plywood, and freeway loop-de-loops.) Patterns and textures throughout the house and site constantly contrast the irregular with the grid, natural forms with humanmade interpretations.

Above The illuminated interior stands out as vivid blocks of color against the fiber cement siding painted a deep blue-black. The lively pattern of the study on one side is offset by the glow of the all-white bedroom on the other. Just as inside the house, exterior texture is applied selectively, with a balance of plain and patterned or tactile surfaces.

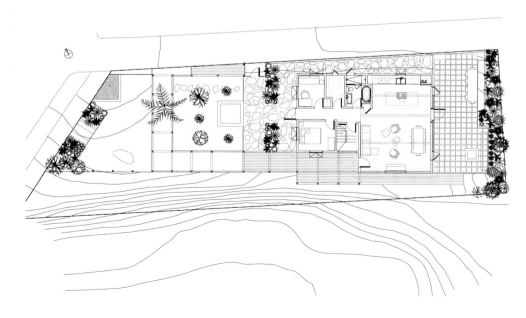

Left Textured surfaces continue outside the house with various hardscape and landscape treatments that improvise on the rectilinear figure of the floor plan. The house joins a series of outdoor rooms consisting of concrete pavers, wood decks, random stone pavers, lawn, reflecting pool, and vegetable garden, along with abundant plantings and an arbor to create a diverse environment with different levels of formality for outdoor living in the warm southern California climate.

Directory of Architects and Designers

Page numbers in parenthesis

Arakawa + Gins
Architectural Body Research Foundation
124 West Houston Street, 4th floor
New York, NY 10012
United States
T 212.674.1393
F 212.674.1624
E revdest@aol.com
www.reversibledestiny.org

Reversible Destiny Lofts, 2005 (100–1, 147–49)*
629 square feet (58.4 square meters) to
760 square feet (70.6 square meters)

Arts Corporation
Mike Latham
39 Great Jones Street, 2nd floor
New York, NY 10012
United States
T 212.979.0315
F 212.254.0545
E info@artscorporation.com
www.artscorporation.com

Home.in.1, 2001 (108–11)
36 square feet (3.3 square meters)

Matthew Baird Design
250 Hudson Street, 11th floor
New York, NY 10013
United States
T 212.334.2499
F 212.334.5721
E mail@bairdarchitects.com
www.bairdarchitects.com

Healy/Kaplow Loft, 2000 (68–71)
1,200 square feet (111.5 square meters)

Shigeru Ban Architects
5-2-4 Matsubara
Setagaya, Tokyo
Japan
T 81.3.3324.6760
F 81.3.3324.6789
E tokyo@shigerubanarchitects.com
www.shigerubanarchitects.com

Glass Shutter House, 2003 (36–39)
residence 92 square meters (990.3 square feet)

Marlon Blackwell Architect
100 West Center Street, suite 001
Fayetteville, AK 72701
United States
T 479.973.9121
E info@marlonblackwell.com
www.marlonblackwell.com

Keenan Tower House, 2000 (20–23, 96–99)
560 square feet (52 square meters)

Barbara Bestor Architecture
3920 Fountain Avenue
Los Angeles, CA 90029
United States
T 323.666.9399
F 323.666.2414
E bestor@mindspring.com
www.bestorarchitecture.com

Echo Park House, 2002 (184–85)
1,200 square feet (111.5 square meters)

Cell Space Architects
Mutsue Hayakusa
3-12-3 Kugahara Ohta-ku
Tokyo 146-0085
Japan
T 81.3.5748.1011
F 81.3.5748.1012
E mutsu@kt.rim.or.jp
www.cell-space.com

Diagonal House, 2005 (32–35, 92–95)
80 square meters (861 square feet)

Fold House, 2004 (160–63)
93.65 square meters (1,008 square feet)

Jonathan Clark Architects
34–35 Great Sutton Street, 2nd floor
London EC1V 0DX
United Kingdom
T 44.20.7608.1111
F 44.20.7490.8530
E jonathan@jonathanclarkarchitects.co.uk
www.jonathanclarkarchitects.co.uk

Flat in Maida Vale, 2001 (76–79)
90 square meters (969 square feet)

Flat in Little Venice, 2002 (158–59)
75 square meters (807 square feet)

Elliott + Associates Architects
35 Harrison Avenue
Oklahoma City, OK 73104
United States
T 405.232.9554
F 405.232.9997
E design@e-a-a.com
www.e-a-a.com

North, 2000 (54–57)
475 square feet (44 square meters)

Endoh Design House
101, 2-13-8, Honmachi, Shibuya-ku
Tokyo 151-0071
Japan
T/F 81.3.3377.6293
E endoh@edh-web.com
www.edh-web.com

Natural Illuminance House, 2001
(41–45, 164–65)
56 square meters (603 square feet)

Jamie Fobert Architects
5 Crescent Row
London EC1Y 0SP
United Kingdom
T 44.20.7553.6560
F 44.20.7553.6566
E mail@jamiefobertarchitect.com
www.jamiefobertarchitects.co.uk

Anderson House, 2002 (46–49)
125 square meters (1,345.5 square feet)

Dick van Gameren Architecten
Barentszplein 7
1013 NJ Amsterdam
Netherlands
T 31.20.530.48.50
F 31.20.530.48.60
E info@vangameren.com
www.dickvangameren.nl

Caruso Apartment, 2002 (112–15)
100 square meters (1,076.4 square feet)

Peter L. Gluck & Partners
646 West 131st Street
New York, NY 10027
United States
T 212.690.4950
E info@gluckpartners.com
www.gluckpartners.com

Scholar's Library, 2003 (17–19)
400 square feet (37 square meters)

Sean Godsell Architects
Level 1 Flinders Lane
Melbourne, Victoria 3000
Australia
T 61.3.9654.2677
F 61.3.9654.3877
E godsell@netspace.net.au
www.seangodsell.com

Future Shack, 2001 (121–23)
15 square meters (161.5 square feet)

Lydia Haack + John Höpfner Architekten
Agnes-Bernauer-Strasse 113
80687 Munich
Germany
T 49.89.123.91.731
F 49.89.589.29.887
E info@haackhoepfner.com
www.haackhoepfner.com
www.microcompacthome.com

micro-compact home, 2005 (116–19)
7 square meters (75.4 square feet)

Henning Larsens Tegnestue
Vesterbrogade 76
DK 1620 Copenhagen V
Denmark
T 45.82.333.000
F 45.82.333.099
E hlt@hlt.dk
www.hlt.dk

Summer House and Studio, 2000 (58–61)
100 square meters (1,076.4 square feet)

Roger Hirsch Architect
91 Crosby Street
New York, NY 10012
United States
T 212.219.2609
F 212.219.2767
E roger@rogerhirsch.com;
www.rogerhirsch.com

Home/Office for a Graphic Designer, 2000
(80–83)
600 square feet (55.7 square meters)

Horden Cherry Lee Architects
Richard Horden, Stephen Cherry, and Billy Lee
34 Bruton Place
London W1J 6NR
United Kingdom
T 44.20.7495.4119
F 44.20.7493.7162
E info@hcla.co.uk
www.hcla.co.uk
www.microcompacthome.com

micro-compact home, 2005 (116–19)
7 square meters (75.4 square feet)

i29 Office for Spatial Design
Jeroen Dellensen and Jaspar Jansen
Industrieweg 29
1115 AD Duivendrecht
Netherlands
T 31.20.695.61.20
F 31.20.416.57.05
E info@i29.nl
www.i29.nl

Fagelstraat Apartment, 2004 (138–41)
55 square meters (592 square feet)

Kempenlaan Apartment, 2002 (72–75)
80 square meters (861.1 square feet)

Masahiro Ikeda
201 Silhouette-Ohyamacho 1-20, Ohyama-cho
Shibuya
Tokyo 151-0065
Japan
T 81.3.5738.5564
F 81.3.5738.5565
E info@miascoltd.net
www.miascoltd.net

Natural Illuminance House, 2001
(41-45, 164–65)
56 square meters (602.8 square feet)

Kanner Architects
1558 10th Street
Santa Monica, CA 90401
United States
T 310.451.5400
F 310.451.5440
E info@kannerarch.com
www.kannerarch.com

Canyon View Office/Guesthouse, 2004
(174–77)
1,000 square feet (93 square meters)

LOT-EK
Giuseppe Lignano and Ada Tolla
55 Little West 12th Street
New York, NY 10014
United States
T 212.255.9326
F 212.255.2988
E info@lot-ek.com
www.lot-ek.com

Lignano Studio, 2005 (154–57)
485 square feet (45 square meters)

Maier + Zelter Architects
John Maier and Ulrike Zelter
5808 Balcones Drive, 204
Austin, TX 78731
United States
T 512.450.0121
E info@maierzelter.com
www.maierzelter.com

Ruth Avenue, 2003 (136–37)
700 square feet (65 square meters)

noroof architects
Margarita McGrath and Scott Oliver
134 Adelphi Street
Brooklyn, NY 11205
United States
T 347.415.4224
F 347.415.4225
E info@noroof.net
www.noroof.net

Slot House, 2005 (88–91, 178–81)
1,000 square feet (93 square meters)

Pool Architektur
Christoph Lammerhuber, Axel Linemayr,
Evelyn Rudnicki, and Florian Wallnöfer
Weyringergasse 36/1
A-1040 Vienna
Austria
T 43.1.503.82 31 -0
F 43.1.503.82 31 33
E pool@helma.at
www.pool.helma.at

T.O. Penthouse, 1999 (128–31)
18 square meters (194 square feet)

**Kazunari Sakamoto Architectural
Laboratory**
Department of Architecture
Tokyo Institute of Technology
2-12-1 Ookayama Meguro-ku
Tokyo 152-8552
Japan
T/F 81.3.5734.3168
E sa@mail.arch.titech.ac.jp
www.arch.titech.ac.jp/sakamoto_lab

Hut T, 2001 (142–43)
60 square meters (645.8 square feet)

Joel Sanders Architect
106 East 19th Street, 2nd floor
New York, NY 10003
United States
T 212.431.8751
F 212.226.9486
E info@joelsandersarchitect.com
www.joelsandersarchitect.com

Hughston Studio, 2001 (124–27, 182–83)
400 square feet (37 square meters)

Saunders Architecture
Todd Saunders
Vestre torggate 22
NO-5015 Bergen
Norway
T 47.55.36.85.06
F 47.97.52.57.61
E post@saunders.no
www.saunders.no

Summer House, 2003 (24–27)
20 square meters (215.3 square feet)

Kazuyo Sejima and Associates
S A N A A
7-A, 2-2-35, Higashi-Shinagawa, Shinagawa-ku
Tokyo,140-0002
Japan
T. 81.3.3450.1754
F 81.3.3450.1757
E sanaa@sanaa.co.jp
www.sanaa.co.jp

Small House, 2000 (85–87)
77 square meters (829 square feet)

Sivilarkitekt MNAL Tommie Wilhelmsen
Pedersgaten 32
4013 Stavanger
Norway
T 47.91.74.44.76
E tommie@online.no
www.tommie-wilhelmsen.no

Summer House, 2003 (24–27)
20 square meters (215.3 square feet)

Studio Aisslinger
Oranienplatz 4
D-10999 Berlin
Germany
T 49.30.315.05.400
F 49.30.315.05.401
E studio@aisslinger.de
www.aisslinger.de
www.loftcube.net

Loftcube, 2005 (30–31, 132–35)
36 square meters (387.5 square feet)

Studio G+A
Benjamin Ascher and Gideon Gelber
307 West 38th Street, suite 811
New York, NY 10018
United States
T 212.500.1488
F 212.500.1490
E info@studio-ga.com
www.studio-ga.com

Convertible Studio, 2000 (65–67)
530 square feet (49.2 square meters)

tonkin liu
24 Rosebery Avenue
London EC1R 4SX
United Kingdom
T 44.20.78376255
F 44.20.7837 6277
E mail@tonkinliu.co.uk
www.tonkinliu.co.uk

Young House, 2002 (166–69)
88 square meters (947.2 square feet)

Dennis Wedlick Architect
85 Worth Street
New York, NY 10013
T 212.625.9222
F 212.625.8885
E info@denniswedlick.com
www.dennis-wedlick.com

Chelsea Apartment, 2003 (150–53)
900 square feet (83.6 square meters)

Uni Architects
Chaewon Kim and Beat Schenk
15 Clifton Street
Cambridge, MA 02140
United States
T 617.491.4259
F 888.202.7817
E info@uni-arch.com
www.uni-arch.com

15 Clifton Street, 2003 (50–53, 171–73)
700 square feet (65 square meters)

Andrea Zittel
Andrea Rosen Gallery
525 West 24th Street
New York, NY 10001
United States
T 212.627.6000
F 212.627.5450
E andrea@rosengallery.com
www.andrearosengallery.com
www.zitT.org

A-Z Cellular Compartment Unit, 2001–02
(105–7)
32 square feet (3 square meters)

A-Z Homestead Unit, 2001–05 (28–29)
120 square feet (11.1 square meters)

Photographer Credits

Toshi Ando
Page 100

Satoshi Asakawa, Zoom
Pages 32–35, 92, 93, 95, 160–63

Jan Baldwin, Narratives
Pages 76, 77, 79

Sue Barr
Pages 47–49

Andrew Bordwin
Pages 13, 108–11

Earl Carter
Pages 121–23

Chuck Choi
Pages 5, 88, 89, 91

Christopher Dawson
Page 18

Richard Dean
Pages 158, 159

Meghan Duda
Pages 90, 179, 181

Adam Friedberg
Pages 51, 53

Mitsumasa Fujitsuka
Page 143

Peter L. Gluck & Partners
Page 18

Jeff Goldberg, Esto
Pages 55, 57

David Grandorge
Page 46

Hertha Hernaus
Pages 128–31

Hiroyuki Hirai
Pages 36–39

Timothy Hursley
Pages 20–23, 97–99

i29 Office for Spatial Design
Pages 72, 73, 75, 138, 139, 141

Steffan Jänicke
Pages 30, 31, 132, 134, 135

The Japan Architect Co.
Pages 85–87

Richard Johnson
Page 6

Ray Kachatorian
Page 185

Elliott Kaufman
Pages 150–53

Sascha Kletzsch
Pages 116–19

John Edward Linden
Pages 174–77

Jens Lindhe
Pages 11, 58–61

Maier + Zelter
Pages 136, 137

Minh + Wass
Pages 80, 81, 83

Masataka Nakano
Pages 100, 101, 147–49

Ted Ngai
Pages 10, 50, 52, 172, 173

noroof architects
Pages 178, 180

Phillip Oteri
Page 171

Sergio Purtell, Black and White on White
Pages 68, 71

Christian Richters
Pages 112, 114, 115

Andrea Rosen Gallery, New York
Pages 105–7

Andrea Rosen Gallery, New York, and Regen Projects, Los Angeles
Pages 28, 29

Hiroyasu Sakaguchi, A to Z
Pages 41–45, 164, 165

Kazunari Sakamoto Architectural Laboratory
Page 142

Joel Sanders Architect
Pages 124, 127, 182, 183

Todd Saunders and Tommie Wilhelmsen
Pages 24–27

Jason Schmidt
Pages 154–57

Robert Shimer, Hedrich Blessing
Pages 54–57

Jefferson Smith, Arcblue Ltd.
Pages 166–69

Dominique Vorillon
Page 184

Paul Warchol
Pages 17, 19

Acknowledgments

Many thanks to everyone who worked together to make this book come about, especially to Alicia Kennedy, my editor, and designer Chris Grimley; also to Betsy Gammons and Cora Hawks at Rockport Publishers. I am grateful to the designers and architects who contributed to this project and for their generosity in granting me interviews. Without the assistance of those at each office and gallery who provided materials and answered countless questions, this book would not have been possible. To my friends, I owe thanks for their valuable suggestions and to my family, my appreciation for their unconditional support.

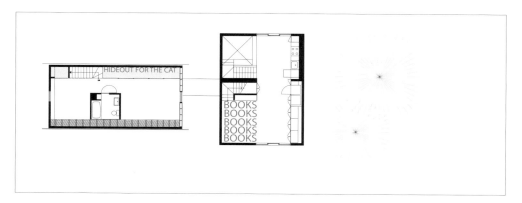

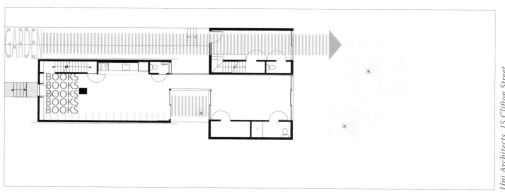

Uni Architects, 15 Clifton Street

About the Author

Yenna Chan has taught design and architectural history and practiced residential architecture in the Boston area. In the past she worked for the architectural journal *Assemblage.* She is now studying toward a Ph.D. in the history of landscape architecture at the Bard Graduate Center in New York.

Dedication
For Rosalie, who perceives every small detail.